SOCIAL JUSTICE PHARISEES

WOKE CHURCH TACTICS AND HOW TO ENGAGE THEM

AD ROBLES

NASHVILLE

NEW YORK • LONDON • MELBOURNE • VANCOUVER

SOCIAL JUSTICE PHARISEES
WOKE CHURCH TACTICS AND HOW TO ENGAGE THEM

Published in New York, New York, by Morgan James Publishing. Morgan James is a trademark of Morgan James, LLC. www.MorganJamesPublishing.com

ISBN 978-1-63195-572-3 paperback
ISBN 978-1-63195-573-0 ebook
Library of Congress Control Number: 2021905104

Cover Design by:
Rachel Lopez
www.r2cdesign.com

SOCIAL JUSTICE PHARISEES

Praise for

SOCIAL JUSTICE PHARISEES

"AD Robles has written a wonderful and very accessible primer on the "woke church" movement filled with helpful examples and biblical engagement. If you have to pick one book to give to your Christian friend who is attracted to the social justice movement, this is the one to give them. A necessary and important work!"

—**Jon Harris**, author of *Social Justice Goes to Church*

For A.J., Ezra and Noah

Table of Contents

Acknowledgments

Angie Kiesling—for editing.

Ben Nash—for reaching out me about doing this book.

Fight Laugh Feast Network—for the many encouragements along the way.

Marcus Pittman—for being the first to make me realize my video content was actually good. (And encouraging me to make it better.)

Morgan James Publishing—for the willingness to take on this important message at this crucial time.

Thanks to the following people for making this book possible and supporting the campaign early on:

Mario Robles—thanks, Dad.

Cody Libolt—you've been a confidant in many ways. Thank you!

Brandon Graves

Christopher Bell

Ed Sanders

J E Myers

Lee Scott Kelley

Matthew Zuehlke
Michael Whipple
Olusanmi Fawehinmi
Robert Lorne
Sam Pauken
Wesley Chandler
Anonymous—I got your back, bro.

Introduction

Take a deep breath and listen to me. You are not crazy. Many possible unique circumstances in your life led you to choose this book and start reading, but ultimately they all amount to the same thing. It feels like an episode of the "Twilight Zone." You woke up one day, and you feel as if you are the same. But everyone else is different.

People you trusted have called you horrible things. Evil names designed to put a black mark on you for life. You do not know why because you don't think you've done anything different or wrong. Old friends you used to hang out with all the time suddenly turn on you and insist you are a racist or white supremacist. Bigot has become something you've grown accustomed to hearing, but it seemingly came out of nowhere. You don't hate any groups of people. At least you don't think you do.

But even beyond personal interactions you have seen a public change happen before your eyes in the space of a few years. It seems as if every ministry, conference series, blog, and parachurch organization you used to glean so much from has changed. They used to be ferocious defenders of the gospel and God's law, but now they are spending much of their time denouncing and lamenting "whiteness" and the "privilege" of the majority culture. You see inordinate amounts of energy spent lamenting female underrepresentation in church leadership. You even see an increasing amount of resources being spent to talk about "sexual minorities" and the oppression members of the LGBT community feel because of the church. The ministry focus has changed, and you can't understand why.

The leaders of these organizations themselves have also changed. Where in the past they had been so encouraging and helpful to your Christian life, now you hear constant words of condemnation. You can see they are angry with the church, but you are not sure why. Some blame the modern white church for killing Martin Luther King Jr. Others claim Christians are bringing in the culture of death and hatred against blacks through their conservative votes. Still others claim racism could be eliminated if only the evangelical church would get on board with fighting against it. They often cite the apparent segregation that marks Sunday morning worship services with shame.

When you look around the church you see blacks, Latinos, Asians and whites worshipping together. Or maybe you don't. Maybe you see lots of white faces, but you can't understand why that would mean the church is given over to racism. You wonder why so many Christian leaders suddenly seem to have angry words and condemnation for you, without even knowing you.

When you take a look at the secular culture more broadly, something else has you even more confused. The language you hear from evangelical leaders and ministries you used to respect as thoroughly biblical, trustworthy, and principled sounds exactly like the language you are hearing from every liberal celebrity, every Christ-hating politician and all manner of pop culture icons you can think of. The message of secular social justice advocacy seems to be in lock step with the message of the woke church which certainly does not seem like it should be the case. The church and world should not be on the same page this much; yet they are.

Worst of all. You have even noticed that some of your most respected Christian leaders and organizations have developed a taste for blaming the church for America's problems. They seem to relish in it. They will get a piece published by CNN.com, Vice, or *The New York Times*, so long as they are willing to trash the church as racists, white supremacists, bigots, killers, haters and even domestic terrorists. The message of the secular culture is clear: "We will offer our huge platforms to any evangelical who will throw the church under the bus." You have watched many leaders whose books you have on your shelf take them up on this deal. You ask yourself, What has happened?

Take a deep breath. I know it feels as if you are going crazy, but you're not. I know how you feel because I have been there.

I will never forget the first time I truly recognized I was in a real fight regarding the woke church (or social justice—I use the terms interchangeably) controversy in the church. I had posted something on social media regarding my being against the public funding for schools based primarily on the skin color demographics of the area. My argument was that schools should not be publicly funded at all, but especially so if it would be done in a partial way according to skin color. Had not anyone ever heard MLK's "I Have a Dream" speech?

By now I am used to this approach, but at the time I was taken aback. I was quickly rebuked by a pastor I respected greatly. This was someone who knew me in real life. This was a mentor of mine. He told me the only reason I had this opinion on school funding was because I was being blinded by "white privilege." This was a surprise to me since I knew for a fact that he knew I was not white.

I do not remember exactly how I responded, because at the time I was not ready for the "not, uh, because you're a racist" style of argument that has become so predictable in our day. Now I have a handful of zings and folders full of memes I can deploy in situations like this in order to "answer a fool according to his folly" in a way that is both entertaining and effective.

Engaging the woke church movement has to be much more than memes and clever zingers. That kind of thing might be enough in woke internet culture, but in the church the stakes are too high. It is a battle over the Word of God. The woke church has created a false religion with a false message and a false plan of salvation. We have a duty before God to grind this movement into dust and make their prophets drink it down. It must be stopped before it rips our churches apart. I've seen the Bible twisted and used in the most grotesque of ways to support social justice policies. Since you have this book in your hands, you likely have as well.

The woke church uses the Bible the way Satan does. They quote it like a book of slogans. When the devil tempted Christ to throw Himself off the temple wall, he quoted two passages.

> *For it is written, He shall give his angels charge over thee, to keep thee: And in their hands they shall bear thee up, lest at any time thou dash thy foot against a stone.*

Christ responded to Satan to correct his attempt to manipulate Him by twisting the Word of God. He responded by reminding him about the law of God that Satan skillfully (and intentionally) left out in his pitch.

> *Ye shall not tempt the LORD your God, as ye tempted him in Massah.*

Satan was not the only one to use the Bible in this way. His children did also. In John 8:44 Jesus called his primary opponents, the Pharisees, Satan's children because of the way they abused the Bible.

> *Ye are of your father the devil, and the lusts of your father ye will do. He was a murderer from the beginning, and abode not in the truth, because there is no truth in him. When he speaketh a lie, he speaketh of his own: for he is a liar, and the father of it.*

He made this connection in a context where he was correcting their slick manipulation of God's word. He refuted their attempts to twist the Scripture with basic and easily understood words from God's law.

It is also written in your law, that the testimony of two men is true. I am one that bear witness of myself, and the Father that sent me beareth witness of me.

This is what we must do. The woke church has followed in the tradition of the Pharisees as they trade in the abuse of Bible passages. To defeat these satanic methods of the woke church we must know the law of God and we must apply it to our modern context. No one can get away with misleading the church if we maintain a laser focus on learning and doing God's commands. We must keep our sword sharp when we confront the errors of the woke church movement.

When you are in a competition of any kind one of the most important pieces of information you can have is insight into how your opponent is planning to fight. This is true whether you are in a sporting event, a fight, a war, or even just an argument. Knowing your opponent's tactics helps you prepare your own and can be the difference between a loss and a victory. Preparation is key.

What follows here is an analysis of what I consider to be the key battlegrounds in the woke church movement. Part 1 is a look at common tactics and arguments used by the woke church movement to push their errors within the church. Like the devil, they misuse Bible verses in their presentations. We will pick the key arguments apart and explore exactly how the verses are being misused. We will follow the example of Christ and remind the woke church of the verses and commands they skillfully left out of their temptations. Consider this section a primer on your opponent's offensive strategy. If you master the tactics the woke church uses, you can mount a seriously effective defense against them.

Part 2 is a list of five verses I believe will help you engage the woke church movement. If your congregation memorizes and fully understands what these verses teach, they will be able to defeat almost all of the woke church's false doctrines. You can use these verses to shut the mouths of the woke church movement before they even get started. Some overlap will take place between the categories and strategies examined in each chapter, and you will need to use wisdom to know when to deploy which attack. I pray you find this book helpful in that mission.

I have heard from many of you over the years. I've heard stories of church splits and controversies. I've heard of pastors and congregants being run out of town. I've heard of once close friends being completely split apart over the topic of social justice. God will defeat this divisive and factious movement. He will do it through a people devoted to understanding His Word and doing His Word. Common people can understand God's commands. May this book help you remind the devil and those who do his work that no amount of Scripture twisting can ever destroy the church of God.

—AD

PART ONE
WOKE CHURCH TACTICS

CHAPTER 1

Do You Even Know about Justice?

(How the Woke Church Attempts to Frame You)

"But let justice roll down like waters, and righteousness like an ever-flowing stream."

—Amos 5:24, ESV

On July 14, 2020, a few weeks after George Floyd died while being detained by a police officer, evangelical author Paul David Tripp uploaded a video to YouTube titled "The Gospel, The Church, And Racial Injustice." In this video Paul pleads with his "white brothers and sisters" to care enough about the issue of racial justice to "just get informed." He suggested four ways to do this. Taking a somber and severe tone he looked into the camera and offered his advice.

> *First, just get out your phone or your iPad or your computer and google "the Bible and justice" and read the volume of passages on this issue. This is one of your Bible's most dominant themes because a God of perfect justice will not be silent in the face of the multitude of injustices that a sin-broken world will create.*[1]

Paul Tripp is correct. If you google the word *justice* in the Bible you will find many, many verses. If you google the very similar word *righteousness* you will find many more. So, for everyone who is planning on deciding whether to join the woke church movement or attempt to defeat it based on how many times the word *justice* is used in the Bible, let me offer my suggestion: Don't make that decision based on something so stupid.

It is difficult to understand how someone so smart can make such a bad suggestion. (I refuse to call this an argument because it is not one; it is a scam.) But he is not the only one. Megachurch pastor Tim Keller also discusses the frequency of the term *justice* in his writings on social justice.[2] Joe Carter, a prolific evangelical blogger, cites Tim Keller to the same effect.[3] (Citing each other in each other's article is one of the best ways to give the appearance of a consensus among authority figures.) The list could go on and on because it is a very popular way to address this topic: "The Bible says the word *justice* an awful lot, therefore…." We will get to that in a moment. Let me show you another tactic of the same kind.

---

1 https://www.youtube.com/watch?v=3CIZ1Omllk8&t=1s
2 https://www.relevantmagazine.com/faith/what-biblical-justice/
3 https://www.thegospelcoalition.org/article/faqs-christians-know-social-justice/

At the 2018 T4G conference, Pastor David Platt gave a speech (or delivered a sermon; I can never tell what to call conference presentations) titled "Let Justice Roll Down Like Waters; Racism and Our Need for Repentance."[4] This was a speech that presented "social justice" as a primary issue of concern for a gospel-centered, Bible-believing church. As you might have guessed, the primary Bible passage he used was Amos chapter 5, starting at verse 18.

In this talk Platt makes the argument that God cares a lot about justice. He cares so much about justice that if you are committing injustice He does not want to hear your songs of praise. He does not even want to consider your sacrifices or offerings. In fact, God cares so much about justice that He gets no pleasure at all from our church gatherings. It all sounds pretty serious, and it is. When you look at the passage he quotes, it seems to make the case pretty plainly.

Verse 18 starts,

> *Woe unto you that desire the day of the Lord! to what end is it for you? the day of the Lord is darkness, and not light.*

Verse 21 and 22 continue:

> *I hate, I despise your feast days, and I will not smell in your solemn assemblies. Though ye offer me burnt offerings and your meat offerings, I will not accept them: neither will I regard the peace offerings of your fat beasts.*[5]

---

4 https://www.youtube.com/watch?v=9o9uHTmnzdY&t=1s

5 https://www.biblegateway.com/passage/?search=Amos+5&version=KJV

And finally, the climax, verse 24:

> *But let justice roll down like waters, and righteousness like an ever-flowing stream. (Amos 5:24, ESV)* [6]

It seems like a pretty open-and-shut case. God reveals in His Word that He cares a great deal about justice. Christians want to be holy as God is holy; therefore we should care about justice. Done deal.

One thing I have noticed over a few years of talking to social justice advocates in the church is that these kinds of arguments are typically used in the beginning of a longer presentation. This is true in all the examples above. Paul Tripp's very first piece of advice, *before you do anything else*, is to google the word *justice* in the Bible. Tim Keller *starts* his article with the statistics on how often the word *justice* occurs in the Bible. Similarly, David Platt's speech on social/racial justice *begins* with a Bible verse that contains the word *justice.* (Just in case anyone is wondering, there is nothing wrong with starting a sermon with a Bible verse.)

What is happening here is that you are being framed. That's right: The woke church movement is attempting to frame you. That might sound nefarious to you, and that's good because it is. Debates are often won or lost, based solely on how the conversation is framed. You must never allow a false framework to stand if you are going to defeat the woke church movement. Allow me to illustrate.

---

6 https://www.biblegateway.com/passage/?search=Amos%205:24&version=ESV

Suppose you are an upstanding American citizen who has never used illicit drugs in your life. One day you get nominated by the president to be the next Supreme Court Justice. Congratulations! Then you remember how confirmation hearings go for conservatives. Not good. They drag you into the interrogation, MSNBC's cameras are rolling, and the judiciary committee sits in gleeful anticipation. As you sit down you are instantly asked the first question.

"Exactly when did you stop using crack/cocaine?"

Most people can see that the way this question is framed is a bit tricky. If you do not answer the question, you look like you are evading. If you do answer the question, then you are admitting that at some point you stopped using an illicit substance, meaning that at some point you were using an illicit substance. This is a simplistic illustration, but the only way to defeat a question that has been framed against you is to challenge the framing of the question itself.

"Mr. Chairman, that question is framed inappropriately. Let it be known that I have never used crack/cocaine; therefore, to ask when I stopped using crack/cocaine is ridiculous."

It is simple enough to spot a question framed against you. Spotting an argument that is incorrectly framed can be a bit more challenging. Let us try a quick warm-up.

In the weeks leading up to the 2020 presidential election many evangelicals attempted to make a pro-life case for voting for Joe Biden. This was weird because Joe Biden was one of the most pro-abortion presidential candidates in history. So how did they make this case? They framed their arguments in a particular way. Evangelicals started arguing that the primary goal regarding abortion was to *limit the number of abortions happening in the United States.* This statement sounds reasonable, and it has an element of truth to it. Who would not want to limit the number of abortions happening? Sit tight for the rest of the argument.

> *Because the primary goal is to limit abortions, then any strategy that accomplishes this task should be allowable for a Christian. Joe Biden favors caring for the poor and marginalized which helps limit abortions through superior contraception services and financial stability. Therefore, voting for Joe Biden could actually help limit abortions more than voting for President Trump despite Biden's pro-choice stance.*

Some will even quote convincing-sounding statistics.

> *If you look at the historical statistics, there are fewer abortions when democrats are in charge; therefore if you want to reduce abortions you will vote democrat.*

Many people will find this line of thinking convincing. I believe this is because of the false, yet reasonable-sounding way the argument is framed.

How do you defeat this? You could try to poke holes in each claim individually. You could challenge the validity of the statistics or challenge the value of studies that show a larger welfare program resulting in fewer abortions. To me, this is like playing whack-a-mole. The more you whack each claim, the more claims keep coming at you. Instead, my recommendation is to cut the argument off at the root. The way the argument is framed is wrong, so challenge that directly.

> *I am a Christian, so while I do want to limit the number of abortions that take place, my highest goal is to honor Christ and love my neighbor according to His commands. Love requires that I defend my preborn neighbor the same way I would anyone else. Murdering them should be illegal under penalty of death. That is what love requires. I personally believe this approach will also limit abortions effectively. Using your framing of "limiting abortions" as the highest goal, one could argue that we should require everyone to be sterilized, since, in theory, that would make the abortion rate zero. I am sure you can see the problem there.*

Before you think to yourself, That's a ridiculous example, do not forget about the way the nation of Iceland was recently celebrated for finding the cure for Down's Syndrome. They simply abort every baby that tests positive and call it a day.

Let us get back to social justice. How are you being framed? In the case of both Paul Tripp and David Platt, it is made clear that their video presentations are targeted for a white audience, white evangelicals specifically. (I guess I am off the hook depending on how you define white.) So the question really is, how are white people being framed by the arguments of the woke church movement?

Think about Paul Tripp's advice in his viral video on social justice. When he recommends you search the phrase "Bible and justice" in Google, what is he assuming about his audience? I think it is clear his expectation is that his audience, in general, is unaware the Bible speaks about justice. His expectation is that when you click the Enter key, the wall of results you get from your keyword search will surprise you to such a degree that you will have to admit you were simply ignorant about the subject of social justice and must now sit at the feet of those pushing the woke church doctrines in order to educate yourself. In fact, only a few sentences later Paul Tripp recommends one of the worst books ever written on the Bible and justice, *Woke Church* by Dr. Eric Mason. Dr. Mason is Paul Tripp's pastor. (Consider checking out the AD Robles YouTube channel for a thorough review and response to this book. I suffered through it so you don't have to.)

Think about David Platt's speech at the T4G conference. When he starts his talk about social justice by quoting the verse

> *But let justice roll down like waters, and righteousness like an ever-flowing stream*

what is he assuming about his audience? I think it is clear he is assuming that the fact God takes justice so seriously will surprise people. Can you imagine? God is so concerned about the topic of justice He actually hates the church gatherings of those who ignore it? David Platt expects this extreme emphasis on justice from the Bible will take his audience off guard. He expects this approach will be enough to shock the system so you will listen and believe the woke church presentation he is about to launch into for the rest of his time on stage. After all, nobody wants to go to church on Sunday if God actually hates your assembly because you *still* do not care enough about justice. Time to get woke, right?

I think both of these are great examples of improper framing. Paul Tripp and David Platt are attempting to make arguments for the woke church in their presentations. Both are presenting ideas of systemic racial injustice, white privilege, and other buzzwords of various kinds. These are extraordinarily complex ideas that are quite difficult for anyone to sell in just one sitting. Both men know this. This is why framing is so important to these discussions in the church.

Is it true that white people, in general, do not realize the Bible speaks often about justice? Is it true, in general, that white people do not realize God cares deeply about the issues of justice? I have no reason to think these are even remotely true.

I grew up in an evangelical church, but I truly came to Christ as an adult. The issues of the law of God, righteousness, justice, and partiality were clearly taught to me from as early as I can remember. I knew justice demanded certain things of me. I knew God cared so much about justice that He sent Jesus to the cross to die for the sins of His people. I knew God did not have different standards of morality for people of different ethnicities or different financial means. I knew from an incredibly early age there was no partiality with God and I should imitate God in this way. All this, with most of my Bible teachers being white evangelicals. I have no reason to think it is true that somehow white evangelicals do not know God cares about justice even though our Bible contains four gigantic books of law. I think this is an absurd assumption on the face of it.

The absurdity of this claim is why it is so important to the woke church to frame it in this way. If you can make someone accept the absurd claim that social justice doctrine was always there, but you simply missed it, then you can fill in the manufactured "void" with all kinds of strange beliefs. In fact, this is exactly what happens in the David Platt T4G speech. It goes like this:

1. Claim that white people have ignored the biblical issue of justice.
2. Quote verses that prove the Bible speaks on issues of justice.
3. Claim that wealth/income disparities (or insert whatever disparity you choose) are part of those issues of justice that have been ignored.
4. Call white people to shrink wealth/income disparities lest they be ignoring the Bible's emphasis on justice.

These steps are oversimplified but do represent the basic format of almost all woke church presentations. Usually emotionally charged stories are sprinkled in regarding past oppression and discrimination. Often they include stories of financial struggle and poverty. Emotions play a big part in every aspect of this, and so people find this basic style of argument convincing. You need to be prepared to stop this line of thinking before it gets rolling because once it is rolling it can be difficult to slow down.

You must challenge the way the conversation is framed at the outset. If I were in a conversation with Paul Tripp or David Platt, it would sound something like this.

> *I appreciate your reminding me of the Bible's emphasis on justice. There is no question that justice is a critical theme of both the Old and New Testaments. But can you help me out? What does that have to do with income disparities? Or what does that have to do with the Michael Brown incident?*

Responses like this serve a dual purpose. First, it establishes a common ground with the woke church. Every Christian ought to be ready to agree the Bible cares about justice. This will completely undercut the false framing of the conversation. We have no reason to assume a Christian of any ethnicity is ignorant of any major theme in the Bible. Responding like this forces them to accept this obvious fact.

Second, it puts the focus of the conversation squarely where it needs to be. We need to be having a Bible study together. We agree the Bible speaks about justice. Great! Now tell me where in that Bible does it charge anyone to eliminate or shrink wealth or income disparities? We agree the Bible speaks about the cause of the poor and the oppressed. Fantastic! So show me where in the Bible it says we assume anytime a violent interaction takes place between a white cop and a black citizen it was motivated by racism. These are the conversations that will eventually lead to the defeat of the woke church movement because the Bible is clear about these issues.

The advocates of social justice sound convincing when they are talking about the concept of justice in an overarching, general kind of way. The minute you insist on biblical defenses of specific ideas and policy claims, things go off the rails very quickly for them. Was Amos talking about income disparities when he prophesied against Israel in his book? I think it would be crazy to argue that he was, which is why David Platt did not go that route. Instead, he attempted to frame you as part of a larger group of evangelicals that have simply not noticed the Bible speaks about issues of justice.

Do not allow an argument to be framed incorrectly. The best way to defeat a social justice argument is to undercut it before it gets any momentum. Sorry, but it is not correct to imply evangelicals did not know the Bible speaks on the issue of justice. We know. We know all too well, which is why we would like to have a Bible study to discuss the details of what biblical justice is. Refusing to allow anyone, even famous evangelical leaders, to frame the justice debate as if we don't already know about the topic of biblical justice is a crucial first step in engaging the woke church movement.

CHAPTER 2
What Is Love?
(How the Woke Church Plays with Definitions)

"Thou shalt not avenge, nor bear any grudge against the children of thy people, but thou shalt love thy neighbour as thyself: I am the Lord."

—Leviticus 19:18

As we have seen, the strategy of framing the topic of justice in an advantageous way is critical to the woke church movement. A lot of time and energy is spent in order to make evangelicals feel as if they have been somehow missing the crucial theme of justice in the Bible so the imaginary "void," created by the way the argument is framed, can be filled with social justice/woke church doctrine. The woke church movement desperately wants to utilize another big theme in the Bible to accomplish their goals. This theme is too big and too obvious to pretend anyone could have missed it for all these years. Nobody would buy that. This is the theme of love.

Love is talked about constantly, and not only in Christian circles. Loving things, loving people, loving dogs, loving morning walks on the beach. Love, love, love. You cannot go five minutes without being assaulted by the concept of love. It is enough to drive a person completely insane. (I'm only half kidding.)

Because it is talked about so often it can be easy to lose track of the actual meaning of the word. The truth of love has been watered down so much by so many people it can sometimes take real effort to keep things straight in our minds.

Here is a cultural truism: love is love. In the United States in 2021 this is truer than any true thing that has ever been true. So is it *actually* true? Well, in a way, yes. I can see the words are identical, so I guess technically I have to agree. But what is it saying? Is the love I have for a good Philly cheesesteak the same as the love I have for my three sons? Well, no, not really. In that case, love really is not love. They are different kinds. Even pagans can understand the difference there.

Is the love a man has for his "legal" husband the same as the love another man has for his legal wife? This one is trickier for the run-of-the-mill pagan. A Christian ought to be able to answer a clear no to this question, since our God has defined what love is in the Bible. (More on this in a moment.) But an unbeliever might struggle a bit here. What really is love? Is love that warm fuzzy feeling you get inside when you think about the other person? I mean, I was raised on the Disney Channel and ABC Family, and so if you go by that, then, yes, love is love.

Is love simply the feeling of affection toward someone? Wanting the best for them? Being willing to consider them and their feelings when you think about yourself and your future goals? I mean, that seems a little less personal, but if you go by that, then, yes, love is love.

Life is always a bit more confusing for pagans. Rejecting the Creator of the universe tends to have that effect on a person's mind. Jesus Christ said He is the Truth, and so to deny Him is detrimental to your ability to know what's what. But unbelievers are not the only ones who can become confused as to what love is.

Allow me to channel my inner Paul Tripp. Try googling "love" and the Bible. You will find a tremendous number of results. This is a topic of great importance to God and no wonder since the Bible tells us, "God is love."[7] Christians know love is a great theme in the Bible, and so it is not possible for the woke church movement to frame their arguments as if Christians didn't know this. What is the next best thing? The woke church movement often tries to confuse the definition of words to make their arguments. They regularly do this with the word *love*.

Celebrity pastor Matt Chandler attempted to trade on this theme during his social-justice-focused speech at the MLK50 conference produced by the Gospel Coalition and the Ethics and Religious Liberties Commission of the Southern Baptist Convention.[8] On the surface, this conference was marketed as a

7 https://www.biblegateway.com/passage/?search=1%20John%20 4:8&version=KJV

8 https://www.youtube.com/watch?v=-wmj0i1oH1Q

celebration of Martin Luther King Jr.'s life, but really it was a coming-out party for the woke church movement in evangelicalism. Like the presentations of David Platt and Paul Tripp in the first chapter, Matt Chandler also makes it clear he considers the target audience of his speech to be white evangelicals. About halfway through his speech he starts reading from Luke chapter 10.

> And behold, a lawyer stood up to put him to the test saying, "Teacher, what shall I do
>
> to inherit eternal life?" And he said to him, "What is written in the law. How do you read it?" And he answered, "You shall love the Lord your God with all your heart, and with all your soul, and with all your strength, and with all your mind, and your neighbor as yourself." And he said to him, "You have answered correctly." ***So...he's got his orthodoxy down.*** But he desiring to justify himself. ***My white brothers and sisters, that sentence is huge.*** But desiring to justify himself, he said to Jesus, "And who is my neighbor?"

He then went on to finish the story of the good Samaritan that we all know and love.

Since in this book chapter 1 comes *before* chapter 2, perhaps you noticed how Pastor Chandler has attempted to frame white Christians here. In the story, the lawyer wasn't loving his neighbor and instead tried to justify himself before Jesus. Big mistake. Just like white brothers and sisters aren't loving their neighbors and instead try to justify themselves, right? I mean, white Christians don't even agree to consider a candidate's skin color when deciding on whom to hire as a pastor. Can you believe that!? (Yes, this is something Pastor Matt Chandler advocates for in the same speech. More on this later.) Don't ever accept the way the woke church movement attempts to frame things unless they provide evidence for what they say.

But this chapter is about definitions, not framing. How should Christians define love? Ironically, Pastor Chandler is in the exact right section of Scripture to define love properly.

When the lawyer challenges Christ, and Christ challenges him right back, some important information is established. The greatest of all the commandments in the law of God is, *"Thou shalt love the Lord thy God with all thy heart, and with all thy soul, and with all thy mind,"* and the second is similar, *"Thou shalt love thy neighbour as thyself"* Elsewhere Jesus adds, *"On these two commandments hang all the law and the prophets."*[9]

Here is part of how Ligonier Ministries describes the implications of what Jesus teaches here:

> *Jesus' answer reveals that love is primarily an action, not a feeling. The commandment to love is an order to do something; thus, we are to love others, serving them even if we do not feel like it. Furthermore, if love for God and neighbor are the commandments upon which the Law and Prophets hang, we cannot somehow separate love from these stipulations and define love in a way that ignores God's law. Any act the Bible forbids is not love; rather, the Law shows us*

9 https://www.biblegateway.com/passage/?search=Matthew%2022&version=KJV

> *how to express true love. Paul can say, "Love does no wrong to a neighbor; therefore love is the fulfilling of the law" (Romans 13:10). He also expects Christians to live out the basic ethical code of the Old Testament. Above all, John Calvin comments, Jesus says that "love is the first and great thing that God demands from us, and therefore the first and great thing that we should devote to him."*[10]

I draw two important facts from Jesus' statement here.

1. Love is an action first and foremost, not a feeling.
2. Love cannot be truly understood outside of the context of God's moral law.

Sorry, Walt Disney. I know this takes some of the magic out of it, but sorcery is a sin anyway; so I guess I'm sorry I'm not sorry.

These two facts must be implanted deep within your soul to have a successful life and to engage in the woke church controversy. "Love is love" might be a technically true statement, but God is the only person who gets to define what love is, and He has. He defines it in His revealed law. Any action or affection that contradicts His law cannot be love no matter how many butterflies it makes you feel in your tummy. Any action that sets aside God's law cannot be love no matter how good your intentions are in the doing. Any attempt at repentance that ignores God's moral law cannot be love no matter how you try to justify it to yourself and your congregation. The law of God is the law of love. That's the

10 https://www.ligonier.org/learn/devotionals/greatest-commandments/

beginning and the end of the discussion. If you want to talk about love, then we must discuss the law of God.

But there is more here. We can draw a third important fact from Jesus' statement. Again, from Ligonier Ministries, this time a guest post by Phil Johnson:

> *What did He mean when He said the two commandments are alike? Well, obviously, they both deal with love. The first calls for wholehearted love toward God, a love that consumes every human faculty. The second calls for charitable love toward one's neighbor—a humble, sacrificial, serving love. Jesus said all the Law and the prophets hang on those two commandments, so the entire Law is summed up in the principle of love. "Love is the fulfillment of the law" (Romans 13:10). Both commandments make that point.*
>
> *But there's another sense in which the second great commandment is just like the first. Loving one's neighbor is simply the natural and necessary extension of true, wholehearted love for God, because your neighbor is made in the image of God.*[11]

So you see it goes beyond simple compliance with God's commands. He wants the affections too. If the command to love your neighbor is like the command to love your God, then that is a command for complete devotion. If you love God with all your heart, soul, mind, and strength, that requires the whole of you. "Every human faculty" is the way Phil Johnson puts it. A

11 https://www.ligonier.org/learn/articles/second-great-commandment/

begrudging obedience to God's law with respect to your neighbor is not going to cut it. Your neighbor bears the image of the one who requires complete love of heart, soul, mind, and strength. Does anybody think an outward obedience without the affections and feelings to match is going to fool God? A third fact about love from this teaching is:

3. Loving your neighbor is intimately connected to loving God first, since your neighbor is made in the image of God.

This is where I think the coffee mug Bible verses about love come into play. Loving your neighbor is not only about the law of God, but it's also about the image of God. How do we treat people in light of the image of God they bear?

> *Love is patient, love is kind, it is not envious. Love does not brag, it is not puffed up. It is not rude, it is not self-serving, it is not easily angered or resentful.*[6] *It is not glad about injustice, but rejoices in the truth. It bears all things, believes all things, hopes all things, endures all things. (1 Corinthians 13:4-7, NET)*[12]

Let's get back to the woke church. The proper definition of love is a critical battleground in the social justice movement. Take

---

12 https://www.biblegateway.com/passage/?search=1%20Corinthians%20 13:4-7&version=NET

a look at this zinger from an article titled *The Fundamentalist War on Wokeness Is a War on Christian Love,* by Michael Bird.

> *Let me be clear, love of neighbour requires you to be concerned for the just treatment of your neighbour, whether they are Black, Hispanic, First Peoples, LGBT, migrant, Muslim, working-class, or even Baptist. Any derogation of a Christian's duty to be concerned about the welfare and just-treatment of their neighbour is an attack on the biblical love command itself.*[13]

Subtle, no? Here's another one, this time from Thabiti Anyabwile of the Gospel Coalition in an article about the social justice debate.

> *At the bottom of the competing ethical visions of Black and White Americans is a deceptively simple but radical command from the Lord Jesus: "Love your neighbor" (Leviticus 19:18; Matthew 22:39; Mark 12:33; Romans 13:9-10).*
>
> *Our practice of neighbor love depends on (1) who we define as neighbors and (2) who we think worthy of our compassion (Luke 10:25-38). If our definition of "neighbor" is small, constricted to only people "like us," then the reach of our compassion will be short. If our definition of "neighbor" is expansive, crossing cultural and ethnic boundaries to include strangers and "the wrong kind of people" like the good*

---

13 https://www.patheos.com/blogs/euangelion/2020/10/the-fundamentalist-war-on-wokeness-is-a-war-on-christian-love/

> *Samaritan, then the reach of our compassion will likewise be expansive.*
>
> *Our conceptions of "neighbor love" determine our political visions and priorities.*[14]

These are typical examples of the kind of rhetoric you can expect to see from the pro-social justice side of the conflict. They make no bones about it. To them, opposing the woke church is opposing love or, at the very least, opposing love for people that are not like "us." This can be effective since Christians are essentially hard-wired to care about love. We have done our Google searches, and we have paid attention in church. We know a Christian should be loving people, even our enemies. But since we haven't lived under a rock for the last fifty years we also know the word *love* is probably the most poorly defined word in the history of everything. Does the woke church movement use the correct definition of love?

Let's start with something that should be an easy one, but sadly is not. In 2018, the same year that at the MLK50 and T4G conferences the woke church started promoting their movement more aggressively, the Gospel Coalition held a women's conference. This is not unusual since the Gospel Coalition holds a lot of conferences; but at this one they were going to do something special. They were going to hold a special fellowship event for "women of color," and they promoted this on their official Gospel Coalition Women's Conference 2018 page. I am unable to link

14 https://www.thegospelcoalition.org/blogs/thabiti-anyabwile/fight-ethics-not/

directly to the advertisement since it's no longer active, but I did cover it in a YouTube video at the time. I include a screenshot of the advertisement around minute 2:18.[15] Here is what the announcement said.

> *Legacy Disciple invites all women of color to a special evening of fun and fellowship on Friday, at 9:30pm. We will engage with a few of our TGCW speakers and also enjoy discussion with one another. Light refreshments will be served.*

Because I was experienced with social justice in the secular world, I instantly knew what this was about. This is a standard practice of social justice advocates. Nothing could be woker than this. In order to achieve racial reconciliation and unity, you must provide separate spaces for people of color where whites are not allowed. I know this sounds stupid, but I had seen this many times before in many different contexts. This was the first time I had seen it in the church, in the context of Christian fellowship, so I called it out immediately.

I was not the only one. This made some waves in evangelical circles, and a number of people called this what it was: segregation. The woke church started noticing the critiques and pushed back. "AD, this isn't segregation," they said. "Nothing in the advertisement says whites cannot come, just that this is focused on the issues people of color face. You're making too much of this. This is not segregation."

---

15 https://www.youtube.com/watch?v=0f-xQ2khf9E

Apparently, the Gospel Coalition caught wind of this oversight in the promotion of the event because shortly thereafter they offered a clarification. Here is what it said:

> *TGCW18 will hold a special Women of Color (WOC) gathering because of those shared, distinct experiences. I understand that many white women attending TGCW18 deeply and sincerely desire to participate in an event like this so they can learn. Praise the Lord! May their tribe increase! However, we run the risk of the audience growing so large (and perhaps even resulting in our sisters of color being the minority at an event specifically designed for them to be the majority) that the goal of cultivating a space for more honest discussion and direct encouragement for women of color would be compromised.*[16]

No more wiggle room. This was intentionally created as a fellowship event at a Christian conference where certain skin colors were not allowed to attend. This was, by definition, a segregated fellowship event promoted at the Gospel Coalition. No whites allowed.

In an article about this insanity, Pastor Tom Ascol quoted a black woman from his congregation that regularly attended Gospel Coalition women's conferences with her white sister. When hearing about the event she said, "I will not go. It is not biblical. Until they can show me from Scripture a divided Christ, I will never consider such a thing. Just wait and see what happens

---

16 https://legacydisciple.org/index.php/2018/06/06/women-of-color-at-tgcw18/

if someone invites me to that meeting and tells me that my sister, Julie, cannot go!"[17]

Straightforward and true. Christ is not divided; therefore Christian fellowship should not be divided. This is basic theology.

In a Twitter tantrum, here is what Thabiti Anyabwile had to say about arguments like this:

> *Do not think it is the gospel or Christian unity you defend if your "defense" lacks compassionate heart, kindness, humility, meekness, patience, bearing with others, forgiveness when you have a complaint, and love.... Some responses from critics claiming to love and defend the gospel fail to exhibit the gospel they claim to love. The integrity and gospel commitment of Christian sisters is being questioned outright simply because they wish to meet together at the invitation of The Gospel Coalition.... Never mind the fact that they will commit themselves to 2.5 days of conference programming and supposed unity. Just consider *one solitary hour together* to care for one another a threat to "gospel unity."*[18]

Pay close attention to how he began his defense of the segregated fellowship event. As we've seen, framing is everything. He starts by listing off the characteristics of love he claims are missing from the critiques offered by those that objected to the event. He pulls some of these directly from the verse in 1 Corinthians 13 quoted above. Love is kind, so he mentions a lack of "kindness." Love is patient,

---

17 https://tomascol.com/tgcw18-a-divided-christ/
18 https://twitter.com/ThabitiAnyabwil/status/1006524742067683329

so he mentions a lack of "patience." Same with "bearing with all things," "humility," "meekness" and "forgiveness." And just so you don't misunderstand him he makes it clear. Those who opposed the Gospel Coalition's segregated fellowship event lacked "love."

He justifies this, in part, by pointing out that the event in question, where white women were not invited, was only "one solitary hour" in the midst of many hours of "supposed unity" at the rest of the conference. How can one hour of segregation threaten "gospel" unity?

Let us run the segregated fellowship event through the three tests of love, cited above:

1. Love is an action first and foremost, not a feeling.

Everything must start here. If you read the Legacy Disciple's defense of this event you will see that the language they use is emotionally charged. If you take the words out of the context of what is actually happening they sound great. They claim "*the goal of cultivating a space for more honest discussion and direct encouragement for women of color....*" Who could oppose such a goal? Elsewhere in the same article they say, "*We hope that this gathering will create a space for women of color to address particular concerns and issues, process them together in small groups, and pray for one another.*" Nothing but good feelings and intentions all around. But we need to have a laser focus on the actions, instead of the feelings. It is not so much about how they *feel* about what they are doing; rather it is about what they are doing. Love is an action first and foremost.

2. Love cannot be truly understood outside of the context of God's moral law.

This is the heart of the issue. Does the Word of God allow for the intentional segregation of Christian fellowship according to ethnicity or skin color? Does He directly forbid it? I think the answer is clear. Not only does God directly forbid such activities through His moral law (James 2:1-4), but we also have examples of believers falling into similar sins of intentionally segregated fellowship and being rebuked for it (Galatians 2:11-13). Regarding Christian fellowship we must strictly defend the truth of Galatians 3, "For as many of you as have been baptized into Christ have put on Christ. There is neither Jew nor Greek, there is neither bond nor free, there is neither male nor female: for ye are all one in Christ Jesus. And if ye be Christ's, then are ye Abraham's seed, and heirs according to the promise."[19] God's moral law clearly does not support, but rather it condemns intentionally segregated Christian fellowship.

3. Loving your neighbor is intimately connected to loving God first, since your neighbor is made in the image of God.

Key to almost all criticisms of the segregated fellowship event was the concern for unity in the body of Christ. If Christ is not divided, how can the fellowship of His body be intentionally divided according to something so ridiculous as skin color? Clearly,

19 https://www.biblegateway.com/passage/?search=Galatians%203&version=KJV

love of God, rejoicing in the truth and rejoicing not in iniquity were at the heart of the objections. How can one say we want a divided fellowship event among those who bear the image of our God, who is not Himself divided? If you consider love of God to be the foundation of loving your neighbor, then a segregated Christian fellowship event is off limits.

By using a biblical definition of love the verdict should be clear. Segregating a fellowship event among Christians is unloving, no matter how good you feel about it. Feelings do not trump actions. This was a decidedly hateful event for the Gospel Coalition to put on.

Let's contrast the event itself with the *response* to this attempt at Christian segregation through the same three tests of love. Thabiti Anyabwile claimed that the response to the event was unloving. We will see.

1. Love is an action first and foremost, not a feeling.

Those who saw the advertisement for the event took action right away. They saw dear sisters in Christ about to commit an act they perceived as sinful according to the Word of God. Pastor Anyabwile is wrong on this. Clearly emotions were involved, but biblical action took precedent.

2. Love cannot be truly understood outside of the context of God's moral law.

Did the response set aside God's law? Leviticus 19 says,

Thou shalt love thy neighbour as thyself: I am the Lord.

We know this passage well enough. But did you know that just one sentence before this, God says,

> *Thou shalt not hate thy brother in thine heart: thou shalt in any wise rebuke thy neighbour, and not suffer sin upon him.*[20]

Love requires action. Love requires you to reason frankly with your neighbor, rebuking when necessary. To allow them to continue in sin without a word is not love. It is definitively "hate" according to God's moral law. According to the moral law, it is not just *allowable* to reason with a neighbor who is about to sin, or currently sinning, but it is *required.* If we love our neighbor, we will commit to rebuke them when necessary. Pastor Anyabwile is wrong on this as well.

3. Loving your neighbor is intimately connected to loving God first, since your neighbor is made in the image of God.

Many of the responses cited a concern for the nature of God. God is not divided, so why should His fellowship be divided? Clearly a love of God seemed to be primary in many people's minds. Again, Pastor Thabiti Anyabwile was simply wrong on this front. Christian fellowship, like all things Christian, should be defined by the book. The book teaches that unity in Christian

20 https://www.biblegateway.com/passage/?search=Leviticus%2019&version=KJV

fellowship is intimately connected to the unity of God. Even the foundations of the response's content was, in fact, loving.

> *That they all may be one; as thou, Father, art in me, and I in thee, that they also may be one in us: that the world may believe that thou hast sent me. And the glory which thou gavest me I have given them; that they may be one, even as we are one: I in them, and thou in me, that they may be made perfect in one; and that the world may know that thou hast sent me, and hast loved them, as thou hast loved me.*[21]

God is love. We know this from the Bible. Love is a central aspect of the Christian life—we know this also from the book. Love is an idea that has been misunderstood and twisted from the very beginning of time—we know this from the book and from experience. When you try to understand love without understanding first who God is and what He is like, all kinds of chaos will be unleashed. You might even be found trying to bring racial segregation back into the church in the name of racial reconciliation and love.

Don't be this stupid. Love must be defined and understood biblically in order to truly be love. Jesus knew this, and He taught this. Love is the most important command of all of God's commands. Love is a *summary* of all of God's commands. We must accept and believe the teaching of our Master if we are going to be doing the works of our Master. We must never allow the woke

---

21 https://www.biblegateway.com/passage/?search=John+17%3A+21-23&version=KJV

church movement to replace a counterfeit, sentimental, feel-good, bogus version of love with the real thing. This is a hill worth dying on. Jesus Christ is the only person qualified to define love, and as His people we must be devoted to the love of Christ alone in order to defeat the woke church movement.

CHAPTER 3
The Government Rests on His Shoulders
(How the Woke Church Is Primarily a Political Movement That Gets Politics Completely Wrong)

"For unto us a child is born, unto us a son is given: and the government shall be upon his shoulder: and his name shall be called Wonderful, Counsellor, The mighty God, The everlasting Father, The Prince of Peace."

—Isaiah 9:6

The woke church movement is a politically motivated movement. Even the most casual conservative observer can tell the woke church promotes clearly progressive policy goals that are given a thin veneer of Christian-sounding words. They try to push these political policy positions as deep theological truths that have somehow been missing from American evangelicalism all this time.

Some are very direct. Here is a tweet from woke "I'm not a Christian rapper" Christian rapper Lecrae.

> *What if the Christians who want to reduce the number of abortions, supported funding healthcare for women, dealt with the systemic racism that creates poverty for women of color, and addressed the income gap between White people and people of color.*[22]

Lecrae is not mincing words. He promotes socialized medicine and socialism in general. He thinks all Christians should. His words are indistinguishable from the biggest leftists that have ever lefted. He actually believes that women kill their babies because they are poor and don't have as much money as other people. Nothing is Christian or true about these ideas. They are pure propaganda.

Some are a little more cunning. Here is Mike Cosper, director of podcasting for *Christianity Today*:

> *Our faith has the deepest resources and strongest foundation to be advocates for human dignity and the protection of women, but our WITNESS has undermined our credibility. We'll pay for this in the generation to come. "Congratulations. You won a Supreme Court seat and*

22 https://twitter.com/lecrae/status/1322959606679769089

> *[maybe] a tax cut. But you lost your prophetic witness and, even worse, you sold your soul."*[23]

Did you vote for the extra bad Republican candidate the TV person told me was very, very bad? Well, congrats! Enjoy your tax cut, you demon! You sold your soul. Everyone knows Democrats stand for human dignity and the protection of women. Subtle.

Still others simply try to create a little space for leftist politics, without coming out full bore in favor of them. Behold the rhetorical wizardry of Timothy Keller.

> *Christians and the freedom of conscience in politics. The Bible binds my conscience to care for the poor, but it does not tell me the best practical way to do it. Any particular strategy (high taxes and government services vs low taxes and private charity) may be good and wise and may even be somewhat inferred from other things the Bible teaches, but they are not directly commanded and therefore we cannot insist that all Christians, as a matter of conscience, follow one or the other. The Bible binds my conscience to love the immigrant—but it doesn't tell me how many legal immigrants to admit to the U.S. every year. It does not exactly prescribe immigration policy. The current political parties offer a potpourri of different positions on these and many other topics, most of which, as just noted, the Bible does not speak to directly. This means when it comes to taking political positions,*

23 https://twitter.com/MikeCosper/status/930436035577876480

> *voting, determining alliances and political involvement, the Christian has liberty of conscience.*[24]

Some people wondered about how he would apply this reasoning to the issue of abortion. His answer would have made Lecrae, the non-Christian, Christian rapper, proud.

> *Some folks are missing the point of this thread. The Bible tells me that abortion is a sin and great evil, but it doesn't tell me the best way to decrease or end abortion in this country, nor which policies are most effective.*

Is the Bible really this unclear about government and politics? Let's think on this a moment.

I will never forget how angry I was when I discovered the truth about the Bible and government. I can't remember the exact book I had finished. More than likely it was a handful of books, articles, videos, and podcasts. But after I found out the truth I was angry about it. Why had no one told me the Bible was so clear about issues relating to the government? Not only does it tell us exactly what God instituted the government to do, but it also gives us a large amount of detailed information on how the government is supposed to do that job. Why had no one told me this before? I wondered.

On my YouTube channel I often say the Bible is way better than anyone has ever told you it is. You just would not believe how much better the Bible is than you think it is. It has value for

---

24 https://twitter.com/timkellernyc/status/1306401474222620672

every single area of a man's life. Not just the big parts of life, but even the small parts of life, the Bible can adequately prepare you for it all. As it happens, the civil government is one of the biggest areas in mankind's everyday life, and, of course, God has much to say about government.

Most people know Romans 13 is the key passage to cite when discussing what the Bible teaches about the Christian's relationship to government. Many have memorized Romans 13:1-2 without even trying.

> *Let every soul be subject unto the higher powers. For there is no power but of God: the powers that be are ordained of God. Whosoever therefore resisteth the power, resisteth the ordinance of God: and they that resist shall receive to themselves damnation.*

This is true and good. Romans 13 teaches that Christians are to submit to the civil government because God Himself ordained it. He established it. Its legitimate power comes from Christ, and we dare not oppose Christ.

But fewer people recognize that Romans 13 also teaches what the ordained role of government is. Here is Romans 13:4-5.

> *For he is the minister of God to thee for good. But if thou do that which is evil, be afraid; for he beareth not the sword in vain: for he is the minister of God, a revenger to execute wrath upon him that doeth evil. Wherefore ye must needs be subject, not only for wrath, but also for conscience' sake. For*

this cause pay ye tribute also: for they are God's ministers, attending continually upon this very thing.[25]

The first thing to notice is that the government is said to be a "minister" of God. Some translations say deacon, or servant. The government is a minister of God in a similar way to how your pastor is a minister of God. They simply have different jurisdictions. Your pastor has authority over the practice and rule of the church, and the government has authority over the practice and rule of civil justice.

As a minister, the government has no authority of its own, outside of the authority God has given it. This is what a minister is. A minister acts on the authority of another. Ministers are only supposed to do the things their master tells them to do. So, just like your pastor cannot assign to himself the authority to discipline your children, since God gave that authority to the parents, the government cannot assign to itself duties or roles God has given elsewhere. A minister has no authority outside of the areas it has been given authority by its sovereign.

Second, we need to recognize the specific role God gives to this specific minister. God gives the government the role of "*revenger*" who is to "*execute wrath upon him that doeth evil.*" This is an extremely narrow role. It is an important role, but it is extremely narrow.

Something often gets lost in our discussions of Romans 13. The duty of the civil government taught in Romans 13 is set up

---

25 https://www.biblegateway.com/passage/?search=Romans+13&version=KJV

in contrast to something else. The end of Romans 12 sets this up for us nicely.

> *Recompense to no man evil for evil. Provide things honest in the sight of all men. If it be possible, as much as lieth in you, live peaceably with all men. Dearly beloved, avenge not yourselves, but rather give place unto wrath: for it is written, Vengeance is mine; I will repay, saith the Lord.*[26]

Do you see how clear the Word of God is here? Romans 12 instructs Christian individuals to never avenge themselves, repaying someone evil for evil. Rather, it says, "*Vengeance is mine; I will repay, saith the Lord.*" But it doesn't leave us hanging regarding what kind of vengeance He has in mind. It is not some kind of mystical, unknowable vengeance done in secret. Not at all! It is vengeance God gives to the civil governing authority to carry out on His behalf. Romans 12 tells us vengeance is the Lord's. Romans 13 teaches us the Lord delegates the authority to take vengeance to the state: "*for he is the minister of God, a revenger to execute wrath upon him that doeth evil.*"

God intends the government's role to be severe, but narrow. We pay taxes to accomplish this task, and we submit to the government in this task because it comes directly from God. The government does not get to assign itself tasks to accomplish as it wills; rather it must stick to the defined roles God has given it. Doug Wilson states,

26 https://www.biblegateway.com/passage/?search=Romans+12&version=KJV

> *Certain things really do belong to Caesar, and other things most emphatically do not. One of the things that does not belong to him is defining what things belong to him.*[27]

The civil government is designed and commissioned to punish evildoers on God's behalf.

Since it is on God's behalf, then it must be done according to God's standard. As we saw in the previous chapter regarding "love," the definitions actually matter a great deal here. Deciding what "evil" is, is critical to finding out who "him that doeth evil" is. As we said in the previous chapter, here we say again: God is the only person who gets to define what evil is, and He has. He defines it in His revealed law. Any government that seeks to define what evil is without the foundation of the Bible is a heathen government in the truest sense of the word.

Further, the government must execute vengeance, as a minister of God, as "*a revenger to execute wrath upon him that doeth evil,*" in the way that God requires it. We would not want to suppose the government does not get to define evil, but somehow does get to define how to punish it. That would not be the proper role of a minister. Rather God, as Sovereign, defines both what evil is and how it should be avenged. The government's role as minister is simply to carry out God's wishes as best they can. Here is Greg Bahnsen on this basic teaching:

> *Since civil rulers are appointed by God, since they bear religious titles, since they are sent to be avengers of*

27 https://twitter.com/douglaswils/status/1291478432094748674

> *God's wrath, since they must punish those who are genuine evildoers, the only proper standard for their rule in society—the only proper criterion of public justice—would have to be the law of God. Those who are ordained by God must obey His dictates, not their own. Those who are called "ministers of God" must live up to such a title by serving the will of God. Those who are to avenge God's wrath must be directed by God Himself as to what warrants such wrath and how it should be expressed. Those who are to punish evildoers must have a reliable standard by which to judge who is, and who is not, an evildoer in the eyes of God. So everything points to the obvious conclusion that the civil magistrate, according to Romans 13:1-7 (even as in the Old Testament), is under obligation to obey the stipulations of God's law as they bear on civil leadership and public justice.*[28]

No, the Bible is not at all unclear about what the government is for and what it is not for. God would not leave us in the dark about ANY good work no matter how small, and the governments of nations are no small thing. From the few verses of Romans 13 we can see that God has a specific plan for governments, and He has specific commands for them to follow. Here are the basics regarding the role of the government according to the Bible:

1. Be a minister of God
2. By executing vengeance on evildoers for God

28 https://www.garynorth.com/freebooks/docs/pdf/by_this_standard.pdf Page 264

3. By defining both "vengeance" and "evildoer" according to God

Let's take a few political proposals from the woke church movement and run them through our three basic rules. To start, we'll let Lecrae speak for the movement. His tweet offers some common policy proposals you'll hear when talking to social justice advocates. This will be a helpful example since he is speaking directly to Christians who, presumably, would want the government to act according to biblical, just, and godly principles. We are going to move quickly to demonstrate how simple this can be. We don't need to overcomplicate these discussions so we won't. Let's start with an easy one.

Abortion

What if the Christians who want to reduce the number of abortions....

Let's stop there and take this piece by piece. Abortion was the primary subject of the tweet. He is addressing people who want to "reduce the number of abortions." A savvy reader will notice the framing of this argument. He starts his argument in a way he believes is to his advantage. To Lecrae, if something can be proven to limit the number of abortions, then it must be better. But an extra savvy reader will refuse to accept the framing. Christians should want God's justice in the case of abortion, whether it limits the number of abortions or not. After all, not allowing people to have sex would limit the number of abortions, but nobody would argue that's a good thing. In any case, if the government executes justice on those who do abortions is it:

1. Being a minister of God?

   Yes. God wants the government involved in justice for murderers. This can be established all the way as far back as Genesis, through the law and prophets and in the New Testament. Sins like this are worthy of the death penalty.
2. By executing vengeance on evildoers for God

   Yes. Abortion is an issue of criminal justice. This is one of the clearest ways God intends the government to act in executing vengeance on evildoers.
3. By defining both "vengeance" and "evildoer" according to God.

   Yes. Death is clearly one of God's primary means of vengeance for those who kill, and people who murder babies are clearly evildoers.

Abortion is clearly a crime God intends the government to involve itself in and execute justice for. But Lecrae doesn't seem to be interested in that. That seems a little too hard-lined and conservative. Let's see what Lecrae imagines as being better alternatives.

Government Healthcare

What if the Christians who want to reduce the number of abortions supported funding healthcare?

Various kinds of healthcare policies are supported by the woke church movement. Whether it is "free" healthcare for all or simply subsidized healthcare for the poor, the woke church movement often advocates for some sort of government intervention to alleviate disparities in healthcare outcomes for Americans. Is this the role of the government? If government is funding healthcare is it:

1. Being a minister of God?

   Yes, I think it is fair to say that helping others through healthcare is something God intends His people to do. Both the Old and New Testaments contain commands that demonstrate God's will here. Caring for the health of sick people is something Christ did and is something we should do. So far so good. Looking after the health of your neighbor is a way to serve God.
2. By executing vengeance on evildoers for God

   Clearly not. Providing healthcare to people can in no way be understood to be executing vengeance of any kind.
3. By defining both "vengeance" and "evildoer" according to God.

   No. See above.

Using our three tests determined from Scripture, healthcare is not a valid role for a just *government* to involve itself in. This is a role for godly *individuals* or the *church*, but not the government.

Poverty

What if Christians who want to reduce the number of abortions...dealt with the systemic racism that creates poverty for women of color?

This one can be a bit trickier. The term *systemic racism* is notoriously squishy. It's the kind of term people use to mean all kinds of scary-sounding things. That being said, systemic racism has been real in the past and could be real in the present. The American slave system was systemic racism. Jim Crow laws were systemic racism. Affirmative action laws are systemic racism, but that's a topic for another chapter. But what Lecrae seems to be interested in here is the result of the supposed "systemic racism": poverty for women of color. (Which itself strikes me as a kind of systemic racism, since white women also live in poverty, but that is a side issue.) If the government seeks to alleviate poverty for women of color, is it:

1. Being a minister of God

   Yes. Caring for the poor is something God intends people to do. This is found in the Old and New Testaments. Jesus commanded it, the apostles did it, and the Bible even has laws for the ancient Israelites to remember in order to provide for needs of the poor. Taking care of the poor is a way to serve God.
2. By executing vengeance on evildoers for God

   No. Giving to the poor is an act of mercy, not vengeance.

3. By defining both "vengeance" and "evildoer" according to God.

    No. See above.

Using our three tests determined from Scripture, alleviating poverty is not a valid role for a just *government* to involve itself in. Again, this is a way for godly *individuals* and the *church* to minister for God, not governments.

Wage/Income Gaps

What if the Christians who want to reduce the number of abortions…addressed the income gap between white people and people of color?

Addressing income gaps is a very popular policy proposal for the woke church. In my experience, when you ask a social justice advocate to define systemic racism or oppression, often they will begin by citing the income or wealth gaps that exist between ethnic groups. The idea being that, since whites and blacks are inherently equal in value, the only thing that can explain an income difference between the two groups is an injustice of some kind. Sounds serious. Some solutions are pure communism: "everyone should have the same income." Some solutions are more modest: "the government should set a minimum wage." Either way, if the government seeks to address the income gaps between white people and people of color, is it:

1. Being a minister of God

    God does require that you pay people their wages on time and according to the agreed upon price. He speaks on this issue in both the Old and New Testaments. But as far as eliminating income gaps and differentials, no, this is not something God expects anyone to do, much less the government.

2. By executing vengeance on evildoers for God

   No. I'm not even sure this one qualifies as mercy, but it's definitely not vengeance. Price setting (or, in this case, wage setting) is not something the Bible commands people to engage in. Prices are to be decided by the two parties involved in the negotiation. No need for the church or government to get involved.

3. By defining both "vengeance" and "evildoer" according to God.

   No. See above.

So, you see, it is pretty simple when you are actually committed to using the biblical model for government. Abortion, since it's murder, is clearly an issue the government needs to be involved in. God's wrath must be executed upon the evildoer that commits murder. But healthcare, poverty and income disparities, though some of them might be good ways to minister for God, are not legitimate things for the *government* to engage in. It is that simple.

At this point someone might accuse me of leaving something out. "AD," they say, "you left out the first part of Romans 13:4."

For he is the minister of God to thee for good.

"A clear case can be made that healthcare is good. Helping the poor is good. Income fairness is good. If the government is a minister for your good, then these things are legitimate for the government to do."

To respond, a quote from David Chilton's fantastic book, *Productive Christians in an Age of Guilt Manipulators:*

> *He must do good. What is "good"? Is God's minister of justice free to decide that for himself? If so, we cannot condemn anything that rulers have done in the past. Hitler regarded the extermination of Jews as good; Nero thought it was a good idea to tax his citizens in order to fund his private orgies and public slaughters; obviously, we could go on and on. Public healthcare, minimum wage laws, and state-financed education may all seem "good" to us; but how can we be sure? There is only one way: we must go, as Isaiah said, "to the law and to the testimony." God's law is "holy, righteous and good" (Romans 7:12; Matthew 23:23). If God's ministers in the state are faithful, they will go to God's Old Testament laws to find out what they should do. Any standard of goodness which is not based on the law of God is not good; it is mere humanism. A state that departs from God's standard is engaged in a vain and cursed attempt to deify itself.*[29]

I'm not sure anyone has said it better than this.

One thing to notice about the failed (from a Christian perspective) policy examples from Lecrae's political tweet is that

29 https://www.garynorth.com/ProductiveChristians.pdf (page 32)

they seem to follow one of two formulas. That is, the woke church is wrong about government and politics usually for one of two reasons.

The first reason is a confusion between the role of government and the role of the individual. As we have seen the proper biblical role of the government is narrow. Important, but narrow. Punishing evildoers is a big job, no question, but it is limited. Not only is it limited, but it is also exclusive. Romans 12 and 13 make it clear that individuals are not supposed to punish evildoers on their own. Vengeance is God's, and God gives that role to the government exclusively.

But God also gives roles and responsibilities to individuals that are likewise limited and exclusive. Charity is one of these. Charity is a good thing; in fact, it is a great thing! Charity to the poor is a primary way to love your neighbor. Why was the Good Samaritan good? Because he saw a neighbor in need and took responsibility, before God, to take care of his needs until he was healed. He did this at great cost to himself. He did this voluntarily, out of love. If we love God we need to love our neighbor. If we love our neighbor, then we need to treat them how God says we should treat them.

> *He answereth and saith unto them, He that hath two coats, let him impart to him that hath none; and he that hath meat, let him do likewise.*
>
> —Luke 3:11[30]

---

30 https://www.biblegateway.com/passage/?search=Luke%203&version=KJV

Healthcare and poverty are issues that are important to the church. They are a matter of loving our neighbor. But, as we saw in the last chapter, we cannot love our neighbor without first loving God, and so we dare not abandon our role and responsibility before God to the government who is ill equipped to take care of the poor in a biblical way. The woke church regularly confuses biblical commands to the individual as if they were biblical commands to the government. This is not a small mistake, and it does not lead to good results. When you are engaging in the social justice debate, you must keep this in mind.

The second reason the woke church is wrong on politics is due to extreme squinting. That's right, squinting. Try it right now. Go to a window, find some trees and squint at them. What do you see? You see the shape of the tree, sort of. You can kind of make out what a tree is, kind of. But you lose all of the detail. You might be able to talk intelligently about some of the tree's characteristics, like the fact that it's big and green and moves in the wind; but while you're squinting you won't be able to be of more use than that. If you want to understand the tree, then you need to stop squinting and look at it for real.

Lots of evangelical leaders do the same thing with the Bible when it speaks about issues of justice and government. Here are some examples.

Jonathan Leeman, of the highly influential 9Marks parachurch organization, wrote the following in an article titled "When Should Churches Reject Governmental Guidelines on Gathering and Engage in Civil Disobedience?" He wrote this in response to the heavy-handed government actions regarding the coronavirus pandemic of 2020.

> *Governments possess authority, if for no other reason than to preserve human life (see Genesis 9:5-6). They are obligated by God to do so. If temporarily banning all gatherings of a certain size accomplishes that end, they should.*[31]

You may notice he claims here that the government's authority is to "preserve human life" and not "execute vengeance on the evildoer." But let's set aside the framing problem (again!) for argument's sake. He says that Genesis 9:5-6 gives the government the authority to "preserve life" and, by application, the authority to ban worship gatherings if a serious enough pandemic is putting the lives at those gatherings at risk. Here is what Genesis 9:5-6 says:

> *And surely your blood of your lives will I require; at the hand of every beast will I require it, and at the hand of man; at the hand of every man's brother will I require the life of man. Whoso sheddeth man's blood, by man shall his blood be shed: for in the image of God made he man.*[32]

---

31 https://www.9marks.org/article/when-should-churches-reject-governmental-guidelines-on-gathering-and-engage-in-civil-disobedience/

32 https://www.biblegateway.com/passage/?search=Genesis%209%3A5-6&version=KJV

I don't know about you, but even if I squint I can't make this verse say anything about the government banning worship services, even for a pandemic with a greater than 99.8 percent survivability rate. This seems like a straightforward verse about the death penalty for those who commit murder. Right? Well, maybe if you try squinting really, really hard.

Jonathan Leeman joined the hosts of the CrossPolitic television show for an interview.[33] They too were a bit perplexed at his application of Genesis 9 in this article, and they decided to ask some clarifying questions. Things only got worse as they found out more. David Shannon, aka The Chocolate Knox, led the questioning:

> Chocolate Knox: *I'm trying to figure out, how are you making your assessments on the world? Do you think someone who commits murder should be killed?*
>
> Leeman: *Uhhh, I think there needs to be space for that in a government program, so, yes, I am pro-capital punishment.*
>
> So far so good. Knox continued:
>
> Chocolate Knox: *Okay, so you are pro-capital punishment. What about a woman who commits an abortion? Should she face the death penalty?*
>
> Leeman: *Probably not, no.*

How could this happen? How can Jonathan Leeman, a trained Bible interpreter and evangelical leader, on the one hand, think a verse about capital punishment can be applied to prove it is

33 https://www.youtube.com/watch?v=8jD6vIqXgEk&t=2693s

legitimate for the government to ban worship in the face of an arguably mild pandemic, but, on the other, think it doesn't apply to ACTUAL murderers when it so clearly does.

The answer is by squinting. He squints and sees that Genesis 9 is really not about capital punishment in the case of murder; rather it is about protecting human life in a generic sense. God has not spoken on the specific details so much as He has spoken on the general principles. He's left much of the details up to us, and Christians can agree to disagree on the details. Squinting is a powerful method to make the Bible say whatever you want it to say.

Here is another example. Tim Keller, in his article "A Biblical Critique of Secular Justice and Critical Theory," said,

> *Socially institutionalized ways of life become weighted in favor of the powerful and oppressive over those with less power. Examples include criminal justice systems (Leviticus 19:15), commercial practices such as high interest loans (Exodus 22:25-27; Jeremiah 22:13) and unfairly low (James 5:4) or delayed wages (Deuteronomy 24:14-15).*[34]

This short paragraph has problems with almost every single one of the Scripture references. (In addition to the usual framing problem, Leviticus 19:15 is a command against partiality and does not at all claim that institutionalized ways of life automatically become weighted in favor of the powerful

34 https://quarterly.gospelinlife.com/a-biblical-critique-of-secular-justice-and-critical-theory/

and oppressive over those with less power. That's not a critique of critical theory; that is just classic critical theory using a Bible verse out of context in support.) But the most egregious example of squinting is with James 5:4. Tim Keller cites this verse as an example of biblical justice being against "unfairly low wages." Here is what James 5:4 says.

> *Behold, the wages of the laborers who mowed your fields, which you kept back by fraud, are crying out against you, and the cries of the harvesters have reached the ears of the Lord of hosts. (James 5:4 ESV)*[35]

Squint all you want, this will still be a verse about not paying your employees. This is about fraud (or simply stealing), not low wages. Social justice advocates love to pretend the Bible speaks where it doesn't and doesn't speak where it does. A verse that is specifically and straightforwardly about not paying your employees through fraud becomes a verse about unfair wages, in general. God gave us the general category but left it up to us to fill in the detail. That is how it morphs into a verse about unfairly low wages to be rectified (obviously) by state-mandated, minimum-wage laws.

This is the magic of squinting. You squint at the tree, you get the general idea of a tree, and then you fill in the details on your own. The woke church has developed an expertise of squinting hard at verses, gleaning general principles, and pretending that if the general principle fits, then their imagination can fill in the

---

35 https://www.biblegateway.com/passage/?search=james+5%3A4&version=ESV

blanks. That's not how God's law works. You can't interpret the Bible well when you're squinting.

Social justice advocates have been trying to squint like this for a long time. The woke church might be new, but the ideas are not. The book by David Chilton, quoted above, was actually a response book to an early social justice warrior named Ron Sider. He also tried to pretend the Bible didn't address these kinds of political/government issues in detail but only in general principles that allowed us lots of flexibility to accomplish. But now, as then, the answer is clear. David Chilton again:

> *"Oh, yes, it does. The trouble is that Sider doesn't like the Bible's answers."*

Neither does the woke church.

CHAPTER 4: A Fine Way

(How the Woke Church Stretches Biblical Passages beyond Their Limits)

"And he said to them, "You have a fine way of rejecting the commandment of God in order to establish your tradition!"

—Mark 7:9, ESV

The summer of 2020 was a tumultuous one. In addition to the economic lockdowns in response to the coronavirus pandemic, numerous violent protests (otherwise known as riots) broke out in response to a handful of shootings involving police officers and black men. The riots were chaotic and indiscriminate. Neighborhoods and businesses were targeted and destroyed regardless of who owned them. Buildings were burned to the ground, people were beaten and killed, and big box stores were looted, all in the name of justice, love and peace. After all, we were told the protests were "mostly peaceful" despite the millions of dollars of destruction and violence.

You would think it would be quite easy for a Christian minister to condemn such destructive behavior as inappropriate, counterproductive, and deeply sinful, and many did. Still, there seemed to be some hesitation to condemn the riots without some form of equivocation from the woke church movement. In a video that has since been deleted, some employees of Southeastern Baptist Theological Seminary got together to talk about the real causes of violent protests. The website "Reformation Charlotte" saved a number of clips and reported as follows:

> *In June, a group of staff from one of the denomination's most prestigious seminaries, Southeastern Baptist Theological Seminary (SEBTS), along with pastors from Southern Baptist churches, held a discussion where they justified the actions of rioters and anarchists while pointing to "white supremacy" as the underlying cause of their disorderly conduct.*
>
> *In the video below, you can hear Wesley Price say,*
>
> *"Rioting makes sense. It's not right, but makes sense… everyone can get to the point where you're going to rage out… it's the voice of those who had their voice taken away."*
>
> *While acknowledging that the rioting "hurts the cause," these men justified the actions anyways by comparing them to a football player who punches his locker hurting his fist after he*

> *lost a game. "I don't want to demonize and villainize them as if they're just doing this for nothing," and "we understand."*[36]

Angry about white supremacy? Burn down your own neighborhood. It's not right, but we won't villainize you for it. It's the white man's fault.

The most interesting comments about these protests, though, came from Dr. Eric Mason. In a sermon preached on August 23, 2020, on the topic of reparations for black people, Dr. Mason had this to say about the nature of protests:

> *I want to give you something, this for free. Some people don't believe that Christians should protest. Do you know that this reparations was paid because God initiated Moses and the Israelites to protest Pharaoh and Egypt? How did they protest? The ten plagues was protest. When Moses went there and said, "Let my people go," that was the sign. That was the protesting sign. And so with that in mind that is beautiful to me. That we see that this reparations here in this passage is a direct result, listen, of protests. Of vehement protest, what God used the protest and God anointed the protest to break down the leadership, to open their hearts to do what he called them to do because he turned the hearts of the king wherever he wants to.*[37]

---

36 https://reformationcharlotte.org/2020/10/29/vietnamese-southern-baptist-church-burned-down-in-philly-as-sbc-leaders-sympathize-with-rioters/

37 https://www.youtube.com/watch?v=7jwf0o9nYWA

I will have much more to say about this particular sermon in this chapter. But for now I want you to simply think about this story. The exodus and the plagues are a story many Christians have heard hundreds of times since childhood. We know it well. Is there anything in the story that would lead you to think the miraculous plagues God accomplished in response to the long-term enslavement of His people is in any way similar to people burning down their own neighborhoods, including the businesses of their own neighbors, in response to a small number of incidents involving police officers shooting black men? I've thought about it for a long time, and the only answer I can come up with is, no, there isn't. This application is a stretch. A massive, massive stretch.

This kind of massive stretch in biblical application is extremely common in the woke church movement. In this chapter we will show other woke church stretches of biblical proportions, I'll provide some commentary on each, and we will talk about why they do this. (Hint: It's not because they don't know how to interpret the Bible properly.)

Verses for "Racial" Police Shootings

Let's take a quick stroll through a minefield, shall we? Let's unpack the biblical witness on the proper way to lean in and come alongside our black and brown brothers and sisters in Christ when we hear reports of racial incidents of violence involving black bodies and white police officers. (Please excuse the excessive use of evangelical buzzwords in the previous sentence. I am trying to contextualize here.) When one of these incidents gets reported on, you are likely to hear the following Bible verses, misapplied and stretched by the woke church movement:

Mourn with Those That Mourn

Rejoice with them that do rejoice, and weep with them that weep.[38]

In the wake of George Floyd's death I uploaded a video to YouTube called "I Will Not Lament with You." It was primarily about the use of this verse by the woke church movement. If you are reading this book you have probably heard this verse used in this context before. It goes like this:

Step 1: The media portray an incident involving a black person's death at the hands of a police officer as a racially motivated murder. They do this by using a short clip of the incident without context.

Step 2: The media portray black people, in general, as mourning at the oppression they face in life exemplified by this latest death.

Step 3: The media propose highly controversial "solutions" to this "oppression."

Step 4: Someone reasonable says, "Well, hold on a moment. We don't even really know what happened here since we only have a short video clip without context from a media organization that is well known for spinning stories

38 https://www.biblegateway.com/passage/?search=Romans+12%3A15&version=KJV

inappropriately. Besides, the data don't seem to indicate this is a widespread problem, and we have a justice system to take care of these kinds of incidents.

Step 5: Woke Christian preachers simultaneously tear their clothes and cry out in a loud voice, "Mourn with those that mourn!"

The goal behind using this verse in this way is to get you into a hyper-emotional state before you start thinking too much. The idea is to get you to *feel* before you *think*, and in that way encourage you to join the social justice movement in their key assumptions about what our world is like. The woke church movement wants you to feel your way through problems, rather than think your way through them. Here is J. D. Greear, president of the Southern Baptist Convention, and woke church advocate:

> *We know that many in our country, particularly our brothers and sisters of color, right now are hurting. Southern Baptists, we need to say it clearly as a gospel issue: "Black Lives Matter." Of course, black lives matter! Our black brothers and sisters are made in the image of God, and so we are saying we understand that many of our black brothers and sisters have perceived for many years that the due processes of justice have not worked for them as they have worked for others in our country. By the way, let's spare each other the quotation of stats right now. You know, if you talk to some black friends you know that they can tell you about their experiences, and how some of them can be quite different*

> *from others in our country. We want rights and privileges to be extended to everybody.*[39]

Notice, of course, the ridiculous way this is framed. Understand that due process is not working, but spare us the statistics. You aren't against rights and privileges for blacks, are you? Don't you know blacks are made in the image of God?

Well, of course we do know that, and that is exactly why we must hear the statistics and facts. Blacks and whites are both made in the image of God, which is why we cannot think with our hearts alone. We need to figure out what happened before we mourn with mourners. Christians should not be mourning with everyone who mourns; we need to think things through first.

How can I say this? Let's think about the entire verse for a moment. It does command that we weep with those that weep. True enough. But it also commands that we rejoice with those that rejoice. Does any sane person believe that based on Romans 12:15 Christians would be required to rejoice with a Ku Klux Klan member who was pleased with the death of George Floyd, a black man?

No, obviously not. That would be ridiculous. But why not? If we simply applied the same application "Don't think just mourn" to "don't think just rejoice," wouldn't it work? But then, of course, we would be required to do two opposite things at the same time for the same incident. Rejoice and mourn simultaneously. It's a biblical command!

---

39 https://twitter.com/jdgreear/status/1271180624720801803

Here is a biblical principle you should memorize from Greg Bahnsen:

> *God's word does not place us in such a morally impossible position, even in theory.*[40]

He was talking about tithing, but it's a principle that applies to everything. God's commands cannot be rendered absurd. So, if your interpretation of a command would make it literally impossible to accomplish, then your interpretation is wrong. The reason Christians would not be required to rejoice with the Ku Klux Klan is because Christians are not supposed to rejoice in evil. First Corinthians 13:6 says,

> *Rejoiceth not in iniquity, but rejoiceth in the truth.*

This requires a small amount of thinking before you blindly "rejoice with those who rejoice." It requires a commitment not to let emotions drive you, but rather to have self-control and remain soberminded enough to determine what the truth is before you sympathize with another person. This means we cannot set aside the "stats," and we must not simply react to an out-of-context video we see reported on CNN. We need to keep our wits about us if we are to love our neighbor appropriately. Here is John Calvin, on Romans 12:15:

> *Rejoice with those who rejoice, etc. A general truth is in the third place laid down—that the faithful, regarding each other with mutual affection, are to consider the condition of*

40 http://www.cmfnow.com/articles/pc085.htm

> *others as their own. He first specifies two particular things—that they were to "rejoice with the joyful, and to weep with the weeping." For such is the nature of true love, that one prefers to weep with his brother, rather than to look at a distance on his grief, and to live in pleasure or ease. What is meant then is—that we, as much as possible, ought to sympathize with one another, and that, whatever our lot may be, each should transfer to himself the feeling of another, whether of grief in adversity, or of joy in prosperity. And, doubtless, not to regard with joy the happiness of a brother is envy; and not to grieve for his misfortunes is inhumanity. Let there be such a sympathy among us as may at the same time adapt us to all kinds of feelings.*[41]

The key words in this are "*as much as possible.*" It is not possible to rejoice with someone regarding something that should not be rejoiced in. Likewise, it is not possible to mourn with someone regarding something that should not be mourned. This is a great Bible verse to describe the nature of Christian love, but love never sets aside truth. In fact, as we saw in chapter 2, love requires a devotion to God's truth in order to be genuine. Truth is basic to love. Sympathizing with your brother's emotions should come naturally to Christians, but it must never set aside the truth.

So what should a Christian do when CNN shows us a fifteen-second video of an unarmed black man being killed by a police officer and our black and brown brothers in Christ are distraught about it? Here are two biblical suggestions:

41 https://biblehub.com/commentaries/calvin/romans/12.htm

First, I would suggest backing up a few verses from Romans 12:15 and reading the whole passage. Greg Koukl, a well-known Christian apologist, often teaches people to "never read a Bible verse." What he means is that you should rarely read a single Bible verse in isolation, because the real meaning of a single verse can often be misunderstood or lost without proper context. Romans 12:9-14, the immediate context to verse 15, says,

> *Let love be genuine. Abhor what is evil; hold fast to what is good. Love one another with brotherly affection. Outdo one another in showing honor. Do not be slothful in zeal, be fervent in spirit,*[g] *serve the Lord. Rejoice in hope, be patient in tribulation, be constant in prayer. Contribute to the needs of the saints and seek to show hospitality. Bless those who persecute you; bless and do not curse them. (Romans 12:9-14, ESV)*[42]

"Let love be genuine" is a great starting point here. Fake love is not love at all. Genuine love must hate what is evil and cling to what is good. How do you know what is good? Through God's law. God defines what is good and what is evil in His law; and so while all death is lamentable in some respects, not all death is lamentable in the same way. On the one hand, if an evil and violent man ends up killed as he attempts to commit a crime, it is appropriate to feel sad for his family while at the same time being glad his crime was not successful and his reign of terror is over. God's law must be our guide if we are going to show genuine love.

42 https://www.biblegateway.com/passage/?search=Romans%2012&version=ESV

Verse 14 is directly relevant to these kinds of situations as well. "Bless those who persecute you." So often the call to "mourn with those who mourn" is really a euphemistic call to protest police officers, to tear down the systems of Western oppression, and to call people you don't know "racist, white-supremacist, neo-Nazi, MAGA, bigots." If we are going to take Romans 12:15 seriously, and we should, we also need to take Romans 12:14 seriously and think twice before we join the mob condemning the supposed persecutors. Rather we should bless them and love them, according to God's law.

The second suggestion comes from James 1:19.

> *Wherefore, my beloved brethren, let every man be swift to hear, slow to speak, slow to wrath.*[43]

This is more than just a suggestion for believers. This is necessary to a just rule of law. God's law requires that we do not rush to judgment on any matter. The book of James echoes this sentiment from many places in the Bible, such as Proverbs 18:17.

> *The first to plead his case seems right, Until another comes and examines him.*[44]

And even more basic, Deuteronomy 19:15:

---

43 https://www.biblegateway.com/passage/?search=James%20 1%3A19&version=KJV

44 https://biblehub.com/proverbs/18-17.htm

> *One witness shall not rise up against a man for any iniquity, or for any sin, in any sin that he sinneth: at the mouth of two witnesses, or at the mouth of three witnesses, shall the matter be established.*[45]

These are all verses that seek to apply the biblical command against bearing false witness. It's one of the ten commandments, and we need to take it seriously. Christians ought to resist the urge to run with the narrative presented to us by CNN, MSNBC, Fox News, or any media organization about any crime whatsoever, especially those of a supposedly "racially charged" variety. Not only is it wise, but it is required by God. Being quick to listen and slow to speak and slow to anger allows you the important time you need to establish the facts first, before you let your emotions take you for a ride. Be wary of any person who counsels you to set aside facts in order to emote "properly" first. This is not biblical in any way.

Truth before emotion should be the primary focus from Christians when it comes to the supposed "epidemic" of racialized police killings in the United States (the real number of these events is so ridiculously low that scare quotes are absolutely necessary); but too often it isn't.

God Is on the Side of the Oppressed

Another biblical narrative is often used by the woke church movement. It is a consistent theme in the Bible and is succinctly stated regularly in the Psalms. Here is Psalm 103:6:

45 https://www.biblegateway.com/passage/?search=Deuteronomy%20 19%3A15&version=KJV

The Lord executeth righteousness and judgment for all that are oppressed.[46]

And regularly in command form for His people, such as Zechariah 7:10:

And oppress not the widow, nor the fatherless, the stranger, nor the poor; and let none of you imagine evil against his brother in your heart.[47]

And often in the wisdom books from God's Word:

But ye have despised the poor. Do not rich men oppress you, and draw you before the judgment seats?[48]

Through these, and many other verses, the idea is promoted that God is squarely on the side of the oppressed. This is an excerpt from an article on the Patheos blog by "progressive Christian" Sean Graham regarding Bishop Desmond Tutu.

There is one piece of wisdom in particular I'd like to share with you today; it is a quote that Tutu often referred to when speaking with those suffering under the oppression of apartheid and a quote he would speak to those who were the perpetrators of apartheid:

---

46 https://www.biblegateway.com/passage/?search=Psalm%20103&version=KJV

47 https://www.biblegateway.com/passage/?search=Zechariah%207%3A9-10&version=KJV

48 https://www.biblegateway.com/passage/?search=James+2%3A6&version=KJV

"God is always on the side of the oppressed, not because they are inherently better than the oppressor, but rather simply because they are oppressed."

> *Tutu linked this statement with a very deep motivating understanding and that is, to be created in the image of God—which is to be human—is the very cornerstone of our dignity. That anything that oppresses that dignity—humanity—God by God's very nature moves to liberate those who are being dehumanised, devalued or degraded.*
>
> *Imagine a God that is not concerned with who is right or who is wrong in situations. But rather a God who wants freedom and liberty. Who wants anything that pulls away from our inherent beauty to be stopped immediately!*[49]

Apparently God is a God who takes sides, and not so much based on right and wrong. Since we seek to imitate God, perhaps we should take sides too? Here is Gospel Coalition author Thabiti Anyabwile in an article about slavery and the recent social justice/culture wars.

> *Paul identifies himself repeatedly as the prisoner, the bound man, the one without freedom. He could have identified himself as the man of authority, the apostle, the one with right to exert himself over others. He nowhere does. That, I think, is instructive for how Christians should engage discussions involving oppressors and the oppressed. We*

49 https://www.patheos.com/blogs/emergentvillage/2013/02/god-takes-sides/

> *should normally be on the side of the oppressed in the fight for justice.*[50]

At least Pastor Anyabwile had the decency to qualify his statement with "normally." But is this true? Does God choose to take the side of the oppressed more often than not? Does He "take sides"?

The answer, of course is, yes, God does take sides. God sides with the righteous. God is perfectly holy, and so He is also perfectly just. Regardless of a person's economic standing, God is for justice. Regardless of a person's skin color, God is for what is right. Regardless of any category of person we can think up, God is for righteousness regarding that person. God is perfectly holy so truth, justice, and righteousness matter very much to Him. They matter much more than a person's standing in any other category.

When we think about the people the Bible refers to as "oppressed" we understand that something is happening to these people that is not right *according to God's standards.* Oppression can only be recognized according to God's own standards. Consider Zechariah 7:10:

> *And oppress not the widow, nor the fatherless, the stranger, nor the poor; and let none of you imagine evil against his brother in your heart.*

---

50 https://www.thegospelcoalition.org/blogs/thabiti-anyabwile/slavery-and-the-bible-the-perspective-of-this-abolitionist/

The idea of oppression is clearly linked to "imagining evil" against people. In other words, seeking to break God's law in order to hurt others. You cannot oppress someone by treating them according to God's law, only by breaking it. This is a very simple but important fact when deciding whose side God is on.

Consider again James 2:7:

> *But ye have despised the poor. Do not rich men oppress you, and draw you before the judgment seats?*

This time oppression is linked to the practice of the rich bringing lawsuits against the poor in courts. Are we to believe that, in these cases, the rich man has legitimate claims of wrongdoing and that James is saying poor people are not liable for *legitimate* crimes against the rich? Of course not! Then, as now, the rich often used their superior resources and ability to hire great lawyers, bribe officials and sell influence in order to overwhelm their poorer neighbors in court. Oppression, in this case, is linked to a *perversion* of justice Christians ought to condemn. Again, you can't oppress someone by keeping God's law. Only by breaking it.

Last, let's take a look at Psalm 103:6.

> *The Lord executeth righteousness and judgment for all that are oppressed.*

Here, again, oppression is linked to a perversion of justice and righteousness. He takes up the cause of the oppressed, yes. But the cause of the oppressed is to correct violations of his law against them. Violations of God's law are possible no matter who you are. All people are fallen in Adam, and all people must be made alive in Christ, regardless of their status, whether free or slave or Jew or Greek or male or female. So the "cause of the oppressed" is the cause of justice. God's justice. God takes sides, but He very much does so based on the reality of who is right and who is wrong. This is not a blanket support of the "oppressed" no matter what the oppressed do. That would not be holy.

This can be easily understood when you look at how God acts in history. Does God side with *all* oppressed people? Were there any in Egypt who were oppressed that suffered the loss of their firstborn? I think clearly there were. Only those who put the blood on the doorposts of their house were passed over. It didn't matter if you were oppressed; if you did not obey the command, your firstborn would have died. God is for His people. He takes up the cause of the oppressed if their cause is righteous. If the cause of the oppressed is not righteous, then God is against that cause.

Progressive Christians have been attempting to twist the Bible regarding this idea long before the woke church movement existed. Ron Sider was as woke as they came back in the 1980s. He wrote a book advocating Christian socialism called *Rich Christians in an Age of Hunger*. In response, David Chilton completely eviscerated his entire premise in a book called *Productive Christians in an Age of Guilt Manipulators*. Again, I highly recommend it. Here is what he had to say about whose side God is on:

The Bible declares that God is actually against certain poor people. The sluggard, who is lazy and thoughtless about the future, has no claim on God's mercy (Proverbs 6:6-11; 13:4, 18; 19:15; 20:13; 21:25-26; 24:30-34; 28:19). God certainly is not "on the side" of any lawbreakers who happen to be poor. Just as the rich often are tempted to be proud, denying God's goodness, so the poor are tempted to covet the possessions of others and to take God's name in vain (Proverbs 30:7-9). In fact, this is a prominent theme in the biblical definition of God's relationship to the poor man: God promises, "When he cries out to Me, I will hear him, for I am gracious (Exodus 22:27). But immediately God offers this warning: "You shall not curse God, nor curse a ruler of your people" (Exodus 22:28). If we are unjust to the poor, and they cry out to God, He will hear and avenge them and provide for their needs. But a poor man must not curse God, as if He has been unfair in His providential dealings with him; also, he must not revile those in authority over him. These are special temptations to which the poor can easily fall prey, and the poor are sternly cautioned against succumbing to them. Whenever we feel oppressed, we want to lash out at God for dealing us a bad hand. The ungodly poor will blame God for their misfortune, and they are promised nothing but judgment. Any man who blasphemes God, be he rich or poor, is to be put to death (Leviticus 24:13-16). Moreover, the ungodly poor, with their slave mentality, regard the state as their rightful savior; if the ruler does not step in to bail them out,

> *they will curse him as well. God will not hear the prayers of those who thus defy Him and His constituted authority. Emphatically, He is not on their side.*[51]

God is on the side of righteousness. Sometimes that aligns with the cause of the oppressed; sometimes it doesn't. Christians, devoted to truth, must discern the difference.

Greek Widows and Hiring Black Pastors

I referenced Pastor Matt Chandler's speech at the MLK50 conference in chapter 1. In that speech he mentioned his strong desire to hire a black pastor for one of his mega-church campuses. He recalled a conversation with his pastor search-firm/head-hunting company.

> *One of the firm's that's helping us find men said, "Let me ask you a question, Pastor Matt. If we find an Anglo 'eight' and an African American 'seven' which one do you want?" I said, "I want the African American 'seven.'" And he said, "What if we find an Anglo 'eight' and an African American 'six'?" Then I said, "Then give me the Anglo 'eight' because that will look and feel to our people like the kind of tokenism I'm preaching against."*

There's a lot biblically wrong with this strange conversation between a pastor and a staffing firm sales executive. I refer you to

51 http://www.garynorth.com/freebooks/docs/a_pdfs/dcpc.pdf page 95

my YouTube video on the topic to get a fuller critique.[52] For now I'd like to focus on the idea of specifically looking to hire a black pastor. Pastor Chandler is not the only one out there looking to add skin color to the list of requirements for his pastor search. Many churches are looking to add people of color to their church staff directory, so long as that color is not "white."

When pressed on the morality of seeking a specific skin color to lead a church, people often reference a story from the book of Acts, regarding the Greek widows. Here is a particularly humorous example by woke church pundit Ed Stetzer, featured in *Christianity Today,* in an article titled "#HellenistWidowsMatter: A Parable."

> *The Hellenist widows were upset. They were being overlooked—treated unjustly.*
>
> *They did not believe they were valued like the Hebraic widows.*
>
> *It was hard to avoid the racial and ethnic issues of the conflict.*
>
> *The Hebraic widows, who were more ethnically aligned with the majority of the church leaders, were just fine. They did not see the issue. Why were these Hellenists so upset? What's the big deal anyway? A widow is a widow, right?...*
>
> *But the apostles saw a better way because they understood the root of the complaint was legitimate. How did they handle this racial concern?*
>
> *They:*

52 https://www.youtube.com/watch?v=VS36mPZJ-F8

- *elevated and empowered Hellenist leaders, with clearly Greek names like Stephen, Prochorus, Nicanor, and Nicolas*
- *spoke in to the situation and made sure the Hellenistic widows were OK with the solution, making sure it "pleased all the people," including those who felt shut out*
- *were not afraid to say #HellenistWidowsMatter to show that they did indeed think they mattered.*[53]

Let's take a look at what really happened with the Greek widows.

> *And in those days, when the number of the disciples was multiplied, there arose a murmuring of the Grecians against the Hebrews, because their widows were neglected in the daily ministration. Then the twelve called the multitude of the disciples unto them, and said, It is not reason that we should leave the word of God, and serve tables. Wherefore, brethren, look ye out among you seven men of honest report, full of the Holy Ghost and wisdom, whom we may appoint over this business. But we will give ourselves continually to prayer, and to the ministry of the word. And the saying pleased the whole multitude: and they chose Stephen, a man full of faith and of the Holy Ghost, and Philip, and Prochorus, and*

53 https://www.christianitytoday.com/edstetzer/2016/january/hellenistwidowsmatter-parable.html

Nicanor, and Timon, and Parmenas, and Nicolas a proselyte of Antioch: Whom they set before the apostles.[54]

A few things to consider:

First, the issue was clearly a real one. These women were actually being neglected in the food distributions. This wasn't an issue up for interpretation, nor was it an injustice that was simply assumed due to a disparity in representation of Greeks in leadership. This was not simply a matter of perception. This was an issue of real partiality, which is to say it was a matter of God's law being broken. This is not analogous in any way to a supposed disparity in black representation in the leadership of churches. You can't simply assume partiality; you have to prove it.

Second, simply "being Greek" was not one of the qualifications the apostles looked for when choosing people to serve the widows. In fact, the Bible explicitly tells us what qualifications they used in order to select leaders, namely, they were to be 1) men, 2) honest, 3) full of the Holy Ghost, and 4) full of wisdom. Notice that "being Greek" had nothing to do with it. Further notice that these qualifications are very similar to the commanded qualifications in the Bible for choosing elders and deacons in the church. Race is not among those qualifications.

Third, the apostles' actions pleased everyone involved. This is because their wisdom was clearly from God, who does not show partiality. Further, the apostles instructed the disciples to select men from among themselves. This is likely what led to the men chosen being Greek, since this dispute rose from among the Greek Jews. Clearly instructing the people to choose "from among you,"

54 https://www.biblegateway.com/passage/?search=Acts%206&version=KJV

the people who were disputing, was a smart idea. This is very different from what the woke church movement is advocating. Consider Matt Chandler's scheme to hire a black pastor. He is intentionally attempting to bring in someone from the outside, from a completely different context culturally, into his local context. This does not strike me as particularly wise and definitely not something that could be justified using the wisdom of the apostles from Acts 7.

I think it's pretty clear that Ed Stetzer and many others who use this passage to justify unbiblical church hiring practices are abusing the beautiful story of the Greek widows. No matter how hard the woke church tries (even if they squint really hard) they cannot make this story fit their cultural/ethnic engineering project.

Reparations for Black People

Let's return to Dr. Eric Mason's sermon on reparations for black people. In the sermon titled "A Biblical Case for Reparations," Dr. Mason makes the case that blacks in America should be compensated for the crime of slavery. He grounds this argument using the biblical principle of restitution. In the law of God people who committed fraud or stole from their neighbors were forced to pay restitution in proportion to what they stole. There were no prison sentences commanded in the Bible.

Restitution is something we should bring back today. It would be more just, humane, and good to have thieves pay back what they owe, plus interest, to those they stole it from, rather than be incarcerated on the taxpayer dime for an arbitrary amount of time. It would be better for the criminal and the victim. God's law is better than man's law. Restitution is undoubtedly something Christians should practice and advocate for in our legal system, but does the biblical teaching on restitution justify paying American blacks reparations for slavery? Let's take a look at the verses Dr. Mason cites.

The primary story he uses is Zacchaeus. The wee little man himself. This is a well-known story that even has children's songs written about it. Here is what the Bible says in Luke 19:

> *Jesus entered Jericho and was passing through it. Now a man named Zacchaeus was there; he was a chief tax collector and was rich. He was trying to get a look at Jesus, but being a short man he could not see over the crowd. So he ran on ahead and climbed up into a sycamore tree to see him, because Jesus was going to pass that way. And when Jesus came to that place, he looked up and said to him, "Zacchaeus, come down quickly, because I must stay at your house today." So he came down quickly and welcomed Jesus joyfully. And when the people saw it, they all complained, "He has gone in to be the guest of a man who is a sinner." But Zacchaeus stopped and said to the Lord, "Look, Lord, half of my possessions I now give to the poor, and if I have cheated anyone of anything, I am paying back four times as much!" Then Jesus said to him, "Today salvation has come to this household, because he too is a son of Abraham! For the Son of Man came to seek and to save the lost."(Luke 19:1-10, NET)*[55]

---

55 https://www.biblegateway.com/passage/?search=Luke+19&version=NET

Dr. Mason believes this story demonstrates the fact that reparations (which to him are synonymous with restitution) are part and parcel of the message of Jesus. The good news is that Mason is clear to separate what he considers "law" with the "gospel." The case he makes for reparations, using the story of Zacchaeus, attempts to argue that paying restitution is an *outworking* of salvation for a Christian, rather than a *requirement* for salvation. This distinction is important and good. I agree completely. If a Christian owes biblical restitution, he should pay it. His salvation does not depend on this, or any work, but good works are a vital evidence of salvation. If we love Christ, we will keep His commandments, including the commandment to make restitution where it is owed.

On this point, Eric Mason and I agree perfectly. Additionally, if you listen to his sermon, he does a fantastic job explaining the story of Zacchaeus. Eric Mason is great at showing his audience what a Bible text says. He even cites Old Testament laws to show you why Zacchaeus did what he did. Here is Numbers 5:6-7:

> *Tell the Israelites, "When a man or a woman commits any sin that people commit, thereby breaking faith with the Lord, and that person is found guilty, then he must confess his sin that he has committed and must make full reparation, add one-fifth to it, and give it to whomever he wronged." (Numbers 5:6-7, NET)*[56]

56 https://www.biblegateway.com/passage/?search=Numbers+5%3A6-7&version=NET

He also mentions Exodus 22:3-4.

> *A thief must surely make full restitution; if he has nothing, then he will be sold for his theft. If the stolen item should in fact be found alive in his possession, whether it be an ox or a donkey or a sheep, he must pay back double. (Exodus 22:3-4, NET)*[57]

These laws, according to Dr. Mason, add valuable context to the story of Zacchaeus. According to God's law, someone who defrauded his brother, or stole from him, could be required by a judge to make restitution of either 120 percent of the value of what was taken, or even as much as 200 percent depending on the details. That was the letter of the law.

Zacchaeus, on the other hand, was so filled with love and repentance upon receiving mercy from Jesus Christ that he decided to forgo the whole idea of waiting for a judge to make him pay restitution. What's more, he decided to pay back *four times* what he took, going way above what was required by God's law. This was a beautiful display of repentance. He couldn't undo what he had done. But he could try to make up for what he had done by giving back much more than he had taken. I agree with Eric Mason's explanation of what Zacchaues did after receiving mercy from Christ. As I said, Dr. Mason is great at explaining what a text says. Most of the woke church movement is. Where they run into trouble is at the point of application, or what a text "means" for us today.

---

57 https://www.biblegateway.com/passage/?search=Exodus+22&version=NET

Here is Eric Mason's own summary of his application of this Bible story:

> *But one of the things that he wanted to do was…to correct something that he did or that was in connection with him. This is so important, right? So "extort" is an interesting word that will be our exegetical springboard into our understanding of reparations. I hope y'all are tracking with me today because I'm having a good time in the text. "Extorted" means to obtain by coercion or intimidation alternately by defrauding… In other words when a person is extorted they're basically defrauded out of their resources. Because he was a tax gatherer he could say, well, there's a new tax out, and Caesar got this, and he fraudulently took more than he was supposed to…And so extorting means to put pressure on someone for personal gain, to shake someone down, to blackmail them, to harass them, to squeeze resources out of them. It's interesting that this exegetical statement here is powerful because it says to oppress someone and cheating them and extorting him. Well, who's more extorted than black people in America. Black people in America were extorted by Europe…we've been extorted by a substandard form of Christianity; we've been extorted by America. We've been extorted. Why? Because we gave you 256 years of free labor…What's crazy about that reality is that there's no real belief that we've been extorted, but we worked for free.*

The main argument here is that since Zacchaeus willingly made generous restitution to the people he defrauded due to an overflowing love of God and neighbor, then American Christians should be seeking to do the same for the people they have defrauded, namely blacks. According to Mason, blacks were defrauded because of the slave trade of the 1800s and therefore should be paid restitution according to biblical law. This is his "biblical" case for reparations.

Dr. Mason makes a small but absolutely crucial mistake in his attempt to apply the story of Zacchaeus in this way. In the story, Zacchaeus is very clear about who he is going to make restitution to. He says,

> *and if* ***I have*** *cheated* ***anyone*** *of anything,* ***I am paying*** *back four times as much!*

Restitution in this case was paid to the specific people that were cheated. The same is true from each and every law of restitution cited by Mason. Here is the Numbers passage:

> *make full reparation, add one-fifth to it, and give it to* ***whomever he wronged.***

Restitution is given to the one who is wronged. Again, in the Exodus passage:

> *he must* ***pay back*** *double.*

Restitution is a pay back. Back to whom? Back to the person that was wronged. In the Bible, lawful restitution involved the specific parties involved. The one who stole, pays back and makes restitution to the one from whom he stole. These are specific people that are to be involved in this transaction; it can't just be anyone. Europeans, as a whole, cannot be made to make restitution to blacks, as a whole. Rather, specific Europeans, those engaged in fraud or stealing, ought to make restitution to specific blacks, those who were defrauded or stolen from. In this way, the story of Zacchaeus cannot be applied to "reparations for black people."

But it's actually worse than this. Dr. Mason's attempted application actually overturns a very clear commandment of God. Like the Pharisees' evil Corban law, the woke church promoting reparations is "a fine way" of rejecting the commandment of God in order to establish their tradition! In this case, I'm thinking of Deuteronomy 24:16.

> *Fathers shall not be put to death for their children, nor shall children be put to death for their fathers; a person shall be put to death for his own sin.*

This principle is basic to God's law. People are individually responsible for their crimes. You cannot punish someone against their will for crimes they personally did not commit and were not involved in. That would be unjust. If we were to apply Eric Mason's "biblical case for reparations" the way he envisions, we would be blatantly breaking this command. In America, the slave trade ended a long time ago. The slave trade was evil, no doubt. Restitution for the evil was owed, no doubt. But both the perpetrators of this evil and the victims of the evil are long dead. So the only way reparations could be paid now would be to require the "sons" to pay for the sins of the "fathers." There is no other way to do this. For those who have died, vengeance is God's alone. Therefore, reparations for black people due to slavery is completely off the table for anyone who loves God, loves their neighbor, and loves justice. To seek to apply the story of Zacchaeus in this way is a massive stretch, and, unfortunately, it's a stretch that also overturns a basic principle of God's law.

The woke church movement stretches many other passages of Scripture beyond their limits, but for now these will suffice to make my point. One thing I would like to make clear is that I do not believe the woke church movement is bad at reading. On the contrary, I think Eric Mason, Ed Stetzer, Matt Chandler, Thabiti Anyabwile and the rest are all actually quite good at understanding what the Bible says. What they are bad at, however, is application. It is the applications of the passages that get stretched beyond recognition.

In my opinion, this is happening because the woke church often starts with a belief on what is right and wrong, and only then go seeking a text that can be shown to have that application. They think they know, intuitively, what "loving your neighbor" ought to look like. So they seek to create a credible sounding case complete with biblical words and stories to attempt to uphold their views publicly without too much scrutiny. Instead of being willing to derive their beliefs from the text regardless of their presuppositions, they seek to use the text in order to justify their presuppositions.

This is nothing new. In fact, Jesus often confronted a group of religious believers who did the same thing. We will examine this in the next chapter.

CHAPTER 5
Specks and Logs
(How the Woke Church Is Guilty of Everything It Accuses People Of)

"Do not judge so that you will not be judged. For by the standard you judge you will be judged, and the measure you use will be the measure you receive. Why do you see the speck in your brother's eye, but fail to see the beam of wood in your own? Or how can you say to your brother, 'Let me remove the speck from your eye,' while there is a beam in your own? You hypocrite! First remove the beam from your own eye, and then you can see clearly to remove the speck from your brother's eye. Do not give what is holy to dogs or throw your pearls before pigs; otherwise they will trample them under their feet and turn around and tear you to pieces."

—Matthew 7:1-6, NET

This chapter will explore a rule known on the internet as "projection." Jesus knew about this phenomenon many years ago. Social justice advocates often find themselves in the uncomfortable position of being guilty of everything they accuse people of. Let's explore just a handful of areas I have noticed over the years that you need to be prepared for.

Pharisees

In this book, I break a rule I regularly follow for myself in my personal interactions regarding social justice. In my defense, it's not so much a "rule" as it is a "guideline." Allow me to attempt to justify myself before we begin.

In ordinary debates and arguments usually the first person to call the other a "Nazi" loses. It is a well-known meme at this point: "Everyone I don't like is Nazi!" Here is some advice: if you want to turn your opponent's brain off so they won't hear the rest of your argument, call them a Nazi first. This is guaranteed to work every time. Nazism is seen as the worst possible ideology, and so to call someone a Nazi is an attempt to paint them in the worst possible light. It is a charge that is easy to make yet is almost always an extreme exaggeration. If you want to have a good conversation with someone, do not call them a Nazi.

In Christian circles, calling someone a "Pharisee" is analogous to calling them a "Nazi." Being called a Pharisee, in the context of a theological conversation, is the worst possible ideology for a Christian to be compared to, and it usually has the same conversation-stopping result as calling them a Nazi. Perhaps you've even seen the newer meme, "Everyone I don't like is a Pharisee!" Ordinarily, it is a tremendous party foul to bring up Pharisees in a theological debate. As with Nazism, it is a charge that is easy to make, but exceedingly difficult to defend since it's almost always an exaggeration. So the question is, why do I make this claim about the woke church? Let me bring it down to the third-grade level: they started it.

The charge of "Pharisee" is an extremely common and supremely ironic one for the woke church to use. The woke church is always quick to adopt slogans in place of logical arguments. Calling someone a Pharisee is one of the most effective slogans they could use in a Christian context. After all, Jesus Himself battled the Pharisees, so clearly they were an enemy to Christianity. As an obviously biblical enemy, associating a group of Christians with the Pharisees could be an extremely effective tool if done convincingly. So they often try.

Here is a particularly clumsy attempt. During the summer of 2018, a group of conservative Christians crafted a fantastic statement against the social justice (woke church) movement in evangelical circles called "The Statement on Social Justice and the Gospel." In it, they expressed a clear insistence that God, through His Word, should drive our conversation on justice. The Bible is the standard.

> *WE AFFIRM that since He is holy, righteous, and just, God requires those who bear His image to live justly in the world. This includes showing appropriate respect to every*

> *person and giving to each one what he or she is due. We affirm that societies must establish laws to correct injustices that have been imposed through cultural prejudice.*
>
> *WE DENY that true justice can be culturally defined or that standards of justice that are merely socially constructed can be imposed with the same authority as those that are derived from Scripture. We further deny that Christians can live justly in the world under any principles other than the biblical standard of righteousness. Relativism, socially constructed standards of truth or morality, and notions of virtue and vice that are constantly in flux cannot result in authentic justice.*[58]

Immediately sensing trouble, noted woke church advocate John Pavlovitz wrote a response where he claimed, without evidence, that if the authors of the statement were being honest, they should have said,

> *We want a Christianity that secures our privilege, that hordes our power, that doesn't require us to be at all confronted or inconvenienced by Jesus. We will do anything to resist equality, curb diversity, and keep marginalized people where they are—even betray the very heart of the Gospels.*

He said many other insane things, but he reserved his kill shot for the final sentence.

---

58 https://statementonsocialjustice.com/wp-content/uploads/2018/09/SSJG-FINAL.pdf

> *Someone needs to tell these terrified white, Conservative, old men. Just like the Pharisees of Jesus' day—they're missing it.*[59]

Here is a much more effective use of the exact same tactic. Again, in 2018, a resolution was drafted in response to the woke church movement by Southern Baptist pastor Grady Arnold. The resolution spoke of social justice in terms that sought to contrast it with biblical justice.

> *Social justice by definition is based on the anti-biblical and destructive concepts of Marxist ideology, and among other things is interested in redistributing wealth, opportunity, and privileges within society.*

And,

> *Whereas social justice differs from the New Testament in that social justice expresses compassion for certain groups they deem as "victims" while hating those with whom they disagree, rather than following the command of Christ to love everyone, and especially our enemies.*

And,

> *Biblical doctrine and the Christian ethic must be chosen over social justice.*[60]

59 https://johnpavlovitz.com/2018/09/15/the-real-statement-on-social-justice-the-gospel/

60 http://sbctoday.wpengine.com/sbc-social-justice-resolution/#comments

In response, a pro-social justice article by Pastor Corey Fields appeared on baptistnews.com. That article contained the following:

> *In Jesus' long list of woes against the Pharisees and teachers of the law (Matthew 23:13-36), he rebukes them for neglecting "the weightier matters of the law: justice, mercy and faithfulness" (v. 23). There it is: first in a list of the top 3. Jesus was essentially quoting Micah 6:8 in which the prophet says that what the Lord requires of us is to "do justice, love mercy, and walk humbly with your God."*[61]

Fields's use of "Pharisee" is more effective than Pavlovitz's, because he quotes Scripture. But, again, the charge of "Pharisee" was used to bolster his point. Why does the woke church think this is a smart play?

If you ask the typical evangelical what the primary problem with the Pharisees was you would get a range of responses all centered around the idea that they were legalists. Legalism is the enemy of the gospel of grace; therefore Pharisees were the enemy of Christ. According to some, legalism is a kind of hyper focus on the law of God. It is an attempt to meticulously keep God's law in order to earn good standing with him. The idea of the typical evangelical is that Pharisees were so focused on a strict application of the law that they became oppressive to common people. They were so careful to keep God's law that they forgot to love people.

---

61 https://baptistnews.com/article/yes-the-bible-teaches-social-justice/#.X7wWW81KiUl

This theory on what legalism is fits the social justice movement's purposes very well. When you look at the "Statement on Social Justice and the Gospel" and the resolution written by Grady Arnold, both documents assert the priority of biblical law and biblical commands over and against external, socially constructed ideologies. This insistence on God's law being more important than man's law should be uncontroversial for any Christian. Yet it provides an opportunity for the woke church movement to exploit. If it is true the Pharisees' big problem was they were *too* concerned with God's law that they didn't love people, then perhaps the same thing is happening with regard to those insisting on God's law being against the ideas of the social justice movement. Perhaps those of us who stand against the woke church movement are simply too legalistic to care about people the way Jesus did.

The problem with this line of thinking is a basic one. The common understanding of legalism is simply incorrect. The Bible does not present the Pharisees as particularly concerned with God's law. In fact, the Bible presents the opposite.

> *In the same way, on the outside you look righteous to people, but inside you are full of hypocrisy and lawlessness. (Matthew 23:28, NET)*[62]

This makes sense even just using basic logic. How could Pharisees be thought of as being hyper concerned with God's law if they didn't love their neighbor? Loving your neighbor is a critical

62 https://www.biblegateway.com/passage/?search=Matthew+23%3A28&version=NET

part of God's law. Just think a moment and consider the activities of the Pharisees in the Bible. They form conspiracies against Jesus continually by bearing false witness, plotting to commit murder, harboring adulterers and other commandment violations. Clearly, the Pharisees did not have a problem with being too hyper focused on obeying God's law. They regularly and blatantly violated God's law, and they didn't seem particularly concerned about it at all. Their agenda was something else entirely.

Also, strictly keeping God's law cannot be Pharisee-styled legalism, since Jesus Christ strictly kept God's law and He was not a legalist.

> *Do not think that I have come to abolish the law or the prophets. I have not come to abolish these things but to fulfill them.(Matthew 5:17, NET)*[63]

Also, insisting that others keep God's law cannot be Pharisee-styled legalism, since Jesus Christ insisted that others keep God's law and He was not a Pharisee.

> *Go, and sin no more.*[64]

Finally, loving God's law cannot be Pharisee-styled legalism, since Jesus Christ loved God's law and He was not a Pharisee-styled anything.

---

63 https://www.biblegateway.com/passage/?search=Matthew%20 5%3A17&version=NET

64 https://www.biblegateway.com/passage/?search=John+8%3A11&version=KJV

> *If you obey my commandments, you will remain in my love, just as I have obeyed my Father's commandments and remain in his love.*

So what was the problem of the Pharisees? They were lawless, sure; but there were lots of lawless people in Jesus' day. Yet he reserved special rebukes for the Pharisees and their legalism. Here is what Gary Demar, senior fellow at American Vision, says on this topic:

> *Legalism is the adding of basic presuppositions to a faith to make that faith more exclusive or less available to "outsiders" who do not think, act, or believe as do the "true" believers. Legalism is one of many power maneuvers by faith leaders who seek to consolidate religious authority in the hands of a very few.*
>
> *The Pharisees fit this definition as do many modern-day Christians who erect an ethical system that does not comport with the Bible, either by setting aside its ethical demands or by replacing biblical norms with extra-biblical decrees. The Pharisees, contrary to popular opinion, did not keep God's law. They were not "the best people of their day."*[65]

Allow me to summarize. The main problem with the Pharisees was that instead of following the law of God meticulously, the way most people think they did, they either added to the law of God or set aside parts of the law of God. The system of a legalist is not

65 https://americanvision.org/1255/biblical-antidote-legalism/

God's system. It is a man-made system that is intended to appear godly even though it isn't. They did this to give the appearance of authority to a select few people who obeyed their twisted version of God's law. This is why Jesus called the Pharisees lawless. They had a law they followed meticulously, but it wasn't God's law.

Perhaps you see where I am going with this. The Pharisees set up a system that *appeared* godly, but when you peeked behind the curtain it was completely man-made. It was a bamboozle, and it was evil. Jesus expertly explained the scam in Mark 7.

The Pharisees confront Jesus because His disciples did not wash their hands before they ate, according to the tradition of Jewish elders. The implication is that Jesus and His disciples were sinners since they ate with defiled hands. They were, in effect, breaking the law. Jesus directly contradicts this man-made addition to the law of God. He knows this was something that was designed to give the appearance of godliness, but He knew it was a scam. He said,

> *You leave the commandment of God and hold to the tradition of men.*
>
> *And he said to them, "You have a fine way of rejecting the commandment of God in order to establish your tradition! For Moses said, 'Honor your father and your mother'; and, 'Whoever reviles father or mother must surely die.' But you say, 'If a man tells his father or his mother, "Whatever you would have gained from me is Corban"' (that is, given to God)—then you no longer permit him to do anything for his father or mother, thus making void the word of God by your*

tradition that you have handed down. And many such things you do." (Mark 7:9-13, ESV)[66]

The Pharisees did many such things. They claimed they did these things for God. It even appeared to many people that the things they did, they did for God. But Jesus cut through the surface level and got right to the heart of it. Despite what they said and despite what it looked like to others, by setting aside the law of God—as it is written—the Pharisees were lawless and in need of repentance.

Pharisees set aside the law of God in order to pursue what appeared to be holiness. But they were not good at keeping the law of God. Their problem was not that they were too focused on God's Word; rather their problem was the opposite. In the last chapter we discussed how the woke church movement sets aside the law of God when they view "racial" police shootings, when they advocate for reparations and when they consider affirmative action hiring practices. Each of these has an appearance of holiness. Presentations on each of these will even reference the kingdom of God as their motivation. But each of these, just like the Pharisees, makes void the Word of God. The woke church will often accuse others of being Pharisees; yet they are the ones who are truly guilty of the substance of being a Pharisee.

And he said to them, "Well did Isaiah prophesy of you hypocrites, as it is written, 'This people honors me with their lips, but their heart is far from me; 7 in vain do they worship

66 https://www.biblegateway.com/passage/?search=Mark%207&version=ESV

> *me, teaching as doctrines the commandments of men.'"* (Mark 7:6-7, ESV)[67]

The woke church often calls people Pharisees, but they themselves do what the Pharisees did.

Who Is Out of Step with the Gospel?

We've mentioned Pastor Matt Chandler's speech at the MLK50 Conference in previous chapters. Here is a transcript from the end of that talk.

> *In Galatians 2:11-14, where we see Peter, who should have known better, drift back into his foolishness. The Apostle Paul confronts him with these words. "But when Cephas came to Antioch, I opposed him to his face because he stood condemned. For before certain men came from James, he was eating with the Gentiles. But when they came, he drew back and separated himself fearing the circumcision party. And the rest of the Jews acted hypocritically along with him." ... Your people are watching, white pastor, white parent. "But when I saw that their conduct was not in step with the truth of the gospel"... To Paul, this issue is not political; it is tied to the finished work of Jesus Christ, and there's a behavior that is out of step with that gospel of Jesus Christ. And Paul, a Jew among Jews, a super Jew, is not afraid to confront another Jew about a behavior that is out of step with the truth of the*

67 https://www.biblegateway.com/passage/?search=Mark%207&version=ESV

gospel. So I'm here to lovingly point out some steps that are out of step with the truth of the gospel.[68]

What is being said here? Pastor Chandler is making the case that Peter's sinful behavior against the Gentile Christians is analogous to white people's poor behavior against black Christians. I have watched this speech many times, and I recommend you watch it for yourself. Pastor Chandler barely even *attempts* to provide evidence this is the case; he just expects you to accept this accusation. The closest we get is a story about him not having an adequate black history unit in public school and an anecdote about how he gets concerned e-mails the day after he quotes Martin Luther King Jr. from the pulpit. Both are a far cry from refusing to eat with brothers in the Lord because you fear the circumcision party, to be sure. But this does not mean we cannot find an analogy for Galatians 2.

The above transcript comes from minute 27 of Chandler's speech. Less than five minutes prior to this statement is his explanation of his intentional search for a black pastor. If you remember he recalled a conversation with his staffing firm regarding qualifications. If the candidate had black skin, then the qualification threshold was less than if the candidate had white skin.

He said, "Let me ask you a question, pastor Matt. If we find an Anglo "eight" and an African American "seven"

68 https://www.youtube.com/watch?v=-wmj0i1oH1Q

which one do you want?" I said, "I want the African American 'seven.'"

Is this practice "in step with the gospel"? This isn't a rhetorical question. I really want you to think about this and answer for yourself. Is it "in step with the gospel" to engage in church business/hiring according to skin color in this way? We don't have to guess here. Paul tells us exactly what the problem was with Peter's actions. The problem was hypocrisy.

Peter was being a hypocrite. He knew full well that the truth of the gospel applied equally to both Jew and Gentile. He knew God did not show partiality so he should not either. To bring ethnicity back into the equation was sinful hypocrisy. This wasn't new information to Peter; he knew this already. He had preached boldly to Gentiles. In fact, in the early days of the church, Peter saw with his own eyes the Holy Spirit of God fall upon the Gentiles.

> *So Peter opened his mouth and said: "Truly I understand that God shows no partiality, but in every nation anyone who fears him and does what is right is acceptable to him. While Peter was still saying these things, the Holy Spirit fell on all who heard the word. (Acts 10:34-35, ESV)*[69]

Afterward, Peter baptized these Gentiles into the church of God.

> *And he commanded them to be baptized in the name of Jesus Christ. Then they asked him to remain for some days. (Acts 10:48, ESV)*

69 https://www.biblegateway.com/passage/?search=Acts%2010&version=ESV

After this, Peter received criticism for these actions. This criticism is strikingly similar to the situation mentioned in Galatians 2.

> *So when Peter went up to Jerusalem, the circumcision party criticized him, saying "You went to uncircumcised men and ate with them." (Acts 11:2-3, ESV)*[70]

But Peter knew the truth of the gospel, and he withstood the pressure with bold proclamations against those who would seek to bring ethnic partiality back into the mix.

> *As I began to speak, the Holy Spirit fell on them just as on us at the beginning.*[16] *And I remembered the word of the Lord, how he said, "John baptized with water, but you will be baptized with the Holy Spirit."*[17] *If then God gave the same gift to them as he gave to us when we believed in the Lord Jesus Christ, who was I that I could stand in God's way?*[18] *When they heard these things they fell silent. And they glorified God, saying, "Then to the Gentiles also God has granted repentance that leads to life." (Acts 11:15-18, ESV)*

Somehow this same Peter was later able to be convinced to show partiality against the Gentile believers. He knew better, but he returned to wickedness instead of holding onto the truth of the gospel. He was being a hypocrite, and Paul called him out on this. He was out of step with the truth of the gospel.

---

70 https://www.biblegateway.com/passage/?search=Acts%2011&version=ESV

We don't need token diversity hiring in order to be united in the gospel. We don't need affirmative action. We don't need to add skin color to a list of requirements in order to do something for the kingdom of God. Rather we simply need to reject hypocrisy in all its forms. We need to hold fast to the truth of the gospel that our unity is found in Jesus and not in our bloodlines. Our family is God's family and not simply the people to whom we are related. Our people are God's chosen people, not simply those whose skin color proportionally represents an arbitrary ideal set by sociologists and PhDs.

The woke church often accuses people of being "out of step with the gospel," but so many of their positions demonstrate that in fact they themselves are the ones displaying hypocrisy when it comes to the gospel and race.

You Racist!

If you are reading this book, it is highly likely you already know how regularly the accusation of racism gets thrown around. I am going to assume that I do not need to prove to anyone how often the woke church accuses others of being racist since it is probably the primary reason the woke church movement even exists. They love calling people racist.

The accusation of racism has two basic meanings: the traditional meaning and the modern nonsense meaning. The woke church regularly engages in both forms of racism. The modern nonsense meaning has to do with disparities. It is racism if a disparity exists between ethnic groups. Do white families earn more than black families? Racism. Are there more white head coaches in the NFL than black? Racism. Does your favorite ministry have more white members on the leadership team than black? Definitely racism!

The woke church makes accusations of this sort all the time. But they are guilty of the same thing. As of December 31, 2020, the leadership team of "The Witness: Black Christian Collective," a woke church powerhouse, was entirely comprised of black professing Christians. Five out of five, not a single white to be found. Lest you think I am cherry picking, consider the Jude 3 Project, founder of the "Courageous Conversations" conference series. According to their website,

> *Courageous Conversations is Jude 3 Project's annual gathering that pairs black voices trained in conservative and progressive spaces to discuss topics that are relevant for the church and culture.*[71]

I checked the photo gallery, and it is indeed true. Only black people were allowed to participate on stage at the conference. Both of these are bad enough, but I ask you to consider also the words of David Platt, SBC leader and pastor.

> *I want to sacrifice more of my preferences as a white pastor. I need to grow in my laying aside of preferences for members of this body, because I want Christ to be exalted through increasing diversity in our leadership… And I know as a white pastor, I have blind spots, so I am part of the*

71 https://www.courageousconvos.org/about-cc

problem. I need friends and fellow pastors around me from different ethnicities who help me see those blind spots.[72]

Last I checked, David Platt is still the senior pastor of his church and he is still white. Racism, yet again. By now, of course, you realize why I call this the "modern nonsense" meaning of the word *racism*. It actually isn't racism at all. Nothing is wrong with having an all-black leadership team or conference speaking list or a black lead pastor. Just like there would be nothing wrong with an all-white leadership team or conference speaker list or lead pastor. The modern version of racism is clearly nonsense, but the traditional meaning of the word *racism* has some *umph* behind it.

The traditional meaning is simple. This is from dictionary.com.

a belief or doctrine that inherent differences among the various human racial groups determine cultural or individual achievement, usually involving the idea that one's own race is superior and has the right to dominate others or that a particular racial group is inferior to the others.[73]

Now this is a definition we can work with. The belief that a particular racial group is inferior to others. This is an accusation the woke church movement regularly makes, and sadly this is also something the woke church movement regularly engages in.

We've mentioned Dr. Eric Mason a number of times already in this book. If any man embodies the spirit of the woke church

72 https://www.youtube.com/watch?v=UUs5mQ0WBP8
73 https://www.dictionary.com/browse/racism?s=t

movement, it is Dr. Mason. As I mentioned previously, he wrote the book on it. *Woke Church* was a best seller despite its content being horrendous. In a brief speech given at the MLK50 conference in Memphis, Dr. Mason laments the status of the racial conversation in the church. He attributes this to two problems: race fatigue syndrome and white frailty. I'll let Eric Mason explain:

> *How in the world can you go from the earth to the moon and you can't do research on the racial history that we need to fight in this country? I don't want to be traumatized by teaching you history. I want you to grow up in your spiritual maturity and grow up in your faith and go on the sanctifying journey of overriding the patriotic way that we've learned history in America. We have patriotic and triumphalism in the ways that we've learned history. And so when you talk to African-Americans now you have on the one side, you have a white frailty. Then on the other side, you have blacks who are dealing with race fatigue syndrome. So you got race fatigue meeting white frailty. White frailty says that "I refuse to talk about that." Blacks on the other side, "I'm sick of going back and forth with you about it."*

Notice how Eric Mason frames this whole problem. We have white people who are expressing "white frailty" by saying, "I don't want to talk about race stuff." But then we have blacks who are traumatized and tired from answering the endless questions from the whites, so they have "race fatigue." Obviously, this is a bit confusing since on the one hand white people don't want to talk about it, but simultaneously want to talk about it so much that blacks are tired of talking about it. This seems like a contradiction to me.

I think we get a bit of a window into what this is all about as Eric Mason continues. He goes on:

> *But the question is we have to begin in our walk with Jesus Christ to say, "I am not going to let the challenges of what has happened much as I ain't feeling you." Let me tell you right now, multiplicities of Negroes ain't feeling evangelicalism. But one of the things I've been...God's been working on me in my heart is that the root of bitterness sprouting up will defile many. And if I allow myself to stew in my frustration towards whites, Jesus won't be my center. My hatred will.*

Eric Mason admits here that a root of bitterness is in his heart toward white people. In fact, he even correctly characterizes this bitterness according to its biblical definition: hatred. Eric Mason tries to fight against the *hatred* he has in his heart toward white people.

The fact that he fights against it is a very good thing. Every Christian ought to be actively warring against the flesh in whatever way it rears its ugly head. But let's not mince words. Eric Mason is a racist. A racist church leader claiming a position of authority and leadership in the area of racism in the church. To me that doesn't make sense. But, to his credit, he is honest about this, and he professes to be warring against this. The problem is that anyone who listened to this speech would not be wrong in wondering how the battle against this sin of racism is going for Eric Mason. Sadly, it doesn't seem to be going very well at all.

Less than *one minute* later in the same speech he expresses exasperation at the notion that a non-woke black man would be hired into church leadership in an evangelical church. This is a direct quote from that speech:

> *But on the other hand, whites have to do this, assume in Jesus' mighty name, that because there is offense, an offense that you need to press into that particular offense and begin to educate yourself on beginning to develop the opportunity to not have reductionistic ways in which you try to cause racial reconciliation like through hiring non-qualified African-Americans to be the multi-ethnic engineers in your local churches. And you know they're not qualified because blacks haven't hired them. And it works against unity when you hire somebody that we not feeling, and you're wondering why multi-ethnicity isn't happening at your church. It's because you have a person that's black on the outside but Angloid on the inside.*[74]

"*Angloid* on the inside." You may not be familiar with this term. When I first heard it I had to look it up. It is a derogatory term for white people. Here is what Urban Dictionary has to say in its entry on "Angloid."

---

74 https://www.youtube.com/watch?v=g9Mv5NJkjJE&t=1s

> *The most stereotypical ugly Englishman. Smelly with a notable lack of teeth. Used as a similar context as mongoloid or negroid. Somewhat similar to a chav. "See that Angloid over there? His teeth look like piano keys."*[75]

Angloid is a racial slur Eric Mason used on stage at a major evangelical event mere seconds after admitting he has hatred in his heart toward white people. But even setting the slur aspect aside for a moment you can see he views being "white" on the inside as a *deficiency* for a black leader. In fact, being too "white" on the inside is a sign of a lack of *qualification* in his mind. After all, how can you hope to achieve racial reconciliation in the church when you have a bunch of black people in leadership at your churches that are really just "Angloids" on the inside?

Dr. Mason is not the only person who thinks and speaks like this within the woke church movement. This is a movement that regularly accuses people of racism, while being racist themselves.

Hypocrisy is rampant in the woke church movement. A pretty safe rule of thumb is to realize that whatever people in the woke church movement accuse you of is likely what they themselves are engaged in. This is especially true when the accusation comes out of nowhere and has no evidence attached to it. Jesus knew this tendency was common to mankind which is why He gave us the warning quoted at the beginning of this chapter, to remove the log from our own eyes before we try to remove the speck out of our brother's. If you are a racist yourself you are not qualified to solve

---

75 https://www.urbandictionary.com/define.php?term=Angloid

whatever racial problems may exist in the church of God. Nobody should listen to your advice. Repent.

Notice what Jesus does not say. He does not say we should not remove the speck out of our brother's eye. Rather, He wants us to be able to see clearly in order to do that difficult work effectively. Call me crazy, but open racists should not be leading a movement against racism in the church unless the goal is to be ineffective. I might be a crazy fundamentalist, but I don't think we should be learning about how to follow God's law from people who regularly disregard God's law in order to look good to others. Perhaps I'm a madman, but I don't think it's very smart to listen to people regarding how to be in step with the gospel when in the same speech they offer racial hiring schemes that so clearly violate the truth of that gospel.

This brings us to part 2 of this book: basic scriptural truths we can commit to our memory and to our lives that show us how to obey Christ in everything we do when engaging the issues the woke church movement promotes. As with everything, the Word of God is the standard.

PART TWO
HOW TO ENGAGE

Chapter 6
The Sin of Partiality—Racism

"You must not deal unjustly in judgment: You must neither show partiality to the poor nor honor the rich. You must judge your fellow citizen fairly."

—Leviticus 19:15, NET

If you are going to engage with the woke church movement at any level it is a great idea to memorize the verse above and its location. It is short, easy to understand and completely devastating to the entire perspective of the woke church and social justice movement. By this I mean this verse by itself can defeat almost any bad idea a social justice advocate can dream up. Before we get into the reasons why I believe this to be so important, let's talk about the verse's context.

Leviticus 18, 19, and 20 are a treasure trove of truth for the modern Christian. In these chapters you will find information regarding both the definitions of sexual immorality and laws against killing children—two of our modern culture's favorite sins. Some attempt to dismiss these kinds of laws since they are contained in the Old Testament; but that becomes less easy to do for a Christian when you realize Leviticus 19 is where we get the command to "love your neighbor as yourself." If Jesus Christ saw this command to have abiding validity for His disciples, then surely we need to take a hard look at the surrounding verses to see what other teachings we can glean from a section of the Bible Jesus quoted so often.

Most important to our discussion is that these chapters also contain information regarding criminal and social justice processes and procedures, which is vital information for any Christian concerned with the topic of justice. Leviticus 19 tells us to reason frankly and not testify falsely as a slanderer. It also tells us to treat foreigners with the same love we would treat a native born. Different people groups were not to have different systems of justice; rather there would be one standard regardless of ethnicity or other factors.

This brings us to verse 15. Clearly a court of law is in focus, but the application goes beyond that immediate context. The purpose of the law is apparent immediately. "You must not deal unjustly...." God is concerned with justice, and what He is about to speak on is something that tends to *pervert* justice.

He continues, "*You must neither show partiality to the poor nor honor the rich.*" The importance of the fact that God mentions both the poor and the rich here cannot be overstated. In those days, same as today, wealth often bought power and influence. Not only did the rich typically have powerful friends that could provide them access to favorable outcomes in court directly, but also the rich, because of their resources, could perhaps be counted on for future favors if a judge ruled their way in a case in the present. The temptation to skew a result in favor of the rich is always there. But that is not the only temptation a court might have to pervert justice.

The poor do not have the same kind of resources or power that the rich do; yet God is just as concerned that nobody shows partiality to them either. Why? The short answer is that God is more concerned with what is true, right, and just than He is with the personalities involved. Rich or poor, native or sojourner, regardless of the demographics, God is completely just. He is no "respecter of persons," as Acts 10:34 puts it.

The longer answer is that the poor have a resource that the rich do not have. They have numbers. More people are in the lower class than are in the higher class; and so a forward-thinking, power-hungry judge might consider showing partiality to the poor in their lawsuits so as to position himself as a "freedom fighter" of sorts. The poor don't have any influence to give out, but they do have bodies to give to the cause. This kind of *human* resource could be tempting for a bad judge to take advantage of by showing partiality to the poor.

In fact, the Bible records a scheme like this. In 2 Samuel 15 the Bible tells the story of Absalom's conspiracy against his father, King David. According to the text, when people would come to the king's court for justice, Absalom would intercept them before they got there. He would tell them,

> *"Look, your claims are legitimate and appropriate. But there is no representative of the king who will listen to you."*[4] *Absalom would then say, "If only they would make me a judge in the land! Then everyone who had a judicial complaint could come to me and I would make sure he receives a just settlement."(2 Samuel 15:3-4, NET)*[76]

The idea here is that these people had legitimate claims, but since they were not powerful, nobody would hear their case. Now we don't know if this was true or not, but Absalom convinced the people it was true, but he was on their side. Why did he do this? The Bible explains:

> *In this way Absalom won the loyalty of the citizens of Israel. (2 Samuel 15:6, NET)*
>
> *Then Absalom sent spies through all the tribes of Israel who said, "When you hear the sound of the horn, you may assume that Absalom rules in Hebron."(2 Samuel 15:10, NET)*

---

76 https://www.biblegateway.com/passage/?search=2%20Samuel%20 15&version=NET

He was a man who desired power. So he became a man that was "for the little guy." He accomplished this by siding with them in their lawsuits against the powerful. This is a powerful temptation for the right person. We see this play out in modern politics regularly.

Regardless of the reasons, though, God is clear. He wants His people to "*judge your fellow citizen fairly.*" That is, to judge people without regard for their demographics but rather according to the law of God. What is right is right regardless of the power differentials involved in the matter. Whether the lawsuit involves people with a lot of power or whether it involves people with a little bit of power, what matters to God, and so what should matter to His people, is what is true and right. This one verse destroys so much of the woke church's primary project.

The sin of racism is the sin of partiality—partiality according to skin color. This means you decide how to judge someone or treat someone not based on how God says you should treat them, but rather according to their skin color. Racism is partiality.

Think about the times you have heard a woke church member advocate policies to address the systemic racism of the past and present. Here is an example from the "about" section of Southeastern Baptist Theological Seminary's "Kingdom Diversity" department website:

> *Who We Are:*
>
> *The Kingdom Diversity Initiative is rooted in Scripture. The biblical story testifies that image bearers ought to reflect the unity and diversity of the Godhead. The fall of Genesis 3*

> *introduced sin into the world and impends the unity of God intended for humanity. The Kingdom Diversity Initiative seeks to heal individual and systemic racial brokenness that causes disunity on our campus, in the church, and society at large. This initiative anticipates the kingdom vision presented in Revelation 7:9-10.*[77]

That sounds pretty good, doesn't it? It certainly seems to check a lot of boxes. Rooted in Scripture? Check! Unity and diversity in the image of God? Check! Healing individual and systemic racial brokenness? Check mate! Who could argue with these kinds of goals? I think most of us can agree the big picture here is noble. Let's take a look at some of the strategies this group employs.

The first thing is scholarships. Southeastern offers a wide variety of scholarships you must be "diverse" in order to obtain. But not all the way diverse, since it excludes white males. That would be too diverse.

> *Student must be from an underrepresented culture or a woman in a doctoral program.*

"Ah," you say, "but white people can get regular scholarships, so it's fine." Right, they can, but so can students "from an underrepresented culture or a woman in a doctoral program." Surely the "regular" scholarships don't ban minorities from them, do they? So they still have access to more because the seminary has decided to practice partiality in their scholarship programs.

77 https://www.sebtskingdomdiversity.com/about

This might not seem like a big deal to you, but I assure you it is. A Christian is not allowed to show partiality in the charity they provide. This is being used as a strategy to combat racism, but it *is* racism. Deciding to give or withhold financial assistance based on skin color is partiality; and it does not matter whether that skin color is associated with a lot of power or a little bit of power. It is wrong. Race-based scholarship schemes should be unheard of in Christian contexts. If you want to reverse your seminary's racist past, my wild idea? Stop being racist. It doesn't work to be racist in reverse. God is not fooled by nonsense like that, and He isn't pleased with it.

But the verse against partiality quoted above has a primary context in the law court. So let's take a look at what "Kingdom Diversity" has to say about criminal justice. One of the primary pillars of the "Kingdom Diversity" department is what they call the "lectern." They believe education and teaching "concrete ways to serve the Kingdom across lines of difference" is critical to fighting racism in our day. I agree, so I clicked the link to their lectern blog. Dear reader, I want you to understand that what I am about to quote is the very first blog article I saw. I did no digging. I did not access the archives. I did not hack into their files. I wouldn't even know how to begin doing such things. This is the very first article I clicked. It is titled "A Beautiful Act of Neighbor Love" and contains the following words:

> *The tragic deaths of George Floyd, Ahmaud Abrery [sic], and Breonna Taylor have reignited the urgency to address the racial injustice in America and offer a ripe moment to practice*

> *the act of neighbor love. These recent events carry the racial overtones that have plagued our country since its inception. Reports indicate the men charged with Arbery's murder used a vulgar racial slur after they fired the fatal shots. Also, action regarding Taylor's death has been slow moving, causing some to lament the lack of justice for black women. George Floyd's death is yet another in the line of black men dying in police custody from what appears to be excessive force.*[78]

As I write, none of the trials where charges have been filed in these killings has even begun. Details that have emerged have been sketchy and conflicting and make assumptions of guilt or innocence by no means clear. In each case, there will be a day in court, and God's law insists that on the evidence of two or more witness will the matter be established. And so, the question must be asked, why is the office of "Kingdom Diversity" assuming injustice in these cases? Likewise, why is this Christian organization assuming each event has "racial overtones." The idea being put forward is that the white people are guilty of murder and they are guilty of murder because they have racial animus toward their victims.

In each of these cases the black person who ended up being killed was involved in some level of criminal activity. This does not mean they deserved to die. It does mean circumstances were in play in each situation that, at the very least, deserve to be heard in open court without partiality. And that is the key. The office of "Kingdom Diversity," in its analysis of a criminal case, is breaking

78 https://www.sebtskingdomdiversity.com/blog/the-beautiful-act-of-neighbor-love

a core law of God. They are deciding a matter, not on the merits of the case, but according to the historic power differentials of white police officers and black people.

They are open about this.

> *These recent events carry the racial overtones that have plagued our country since its inception.*

They are analyzing the current cases against the various police officers through the lens of skin color and race relations throughout the history of the United States. This is the opposite of impartiality. This is the opposite of what Christ requires in court cases. Christians are held to a high standard of justice. Justice must be meted out impartially. This is especially true when you are considering the power differentials at play in court. That is the primary message of Leviticus 19:15. Whether rich and powerful, or poor and powerless, what matters are the facts. We are to judge impartially.

"Ah," you say, "but what you are trying to do is ignore the history of oppression. Yes, ideally we are not to show partiality in these cases, but the years of racism and oppression that blacks have endured in this country color every interaction in the present. We cannot just ignore what happened in the past. Rather we must actively seek to reverse it. That is what repentance is!"

I'm glad you brought up history. God has something to say about historical injustice too.

CHAPTER 7
Historic Oppression Does Not Change God's Commands

"You must not hate an Edomite, for he is your relative; you must not hate an Egyptian, for you lived as a foreigner in his land."
—Deuteronomy 23:7, NET

We have talked about the ways the woke church movement inappropriately uses history to advance their cause. They do this because it is effective. The history of the United States is not always pretty. Even looking at it with rose-tinted glasses it has blemishes; but if the worst of the slave narratives are to be believed, it was sometimes a hell on earth.

But we must consider a historical fact that is regularly glossed over in conversations about racial justice involving the woke church. Slavery was not invented by the United States of America. I know that sounds obvious, but if you gauge by the many woke church conversations about justice, slavery, and the importance of knowing history, you would think you only needed to go back to roughly 1619.

This arbitrary timeline, embraced by much of the woke church, is strategic. If you look into history too far you'll learn that every ethnic group has enslaved other ethnic groups at one time or another. You might even find out such horrors as the fact that black Africans participated in, and profited from, the American slave trade. There is plenty of blame to go around. Slavery even goes as far back as Bible times.

We all know the story of the Exodus. The people of Israel increase in number while they are living in the land of Egypt, and a new king rises up and starts fearing their numbers. As a solution he decides to oppress and enslave the Israelites in order to neutralize them.

The slavery the Israelites endured in Egypt was brutal. The woke church will often try to convince you that old-style biblical slavery was nothing compared to American chattel slavery. You don't need to be a historian to know this is a lie. All you need is the ability to read. In the first chapter of Exodus, the Bible describes their slavery as "bitter," "ruthless," and "oppressive." It also describes Egypt's attempt at genocide, by their plan to literally kill any son born to an Israelite. The Egyptians were attempting to snuff out the nation of Israel from the face of the earth by destroying their bloodline. Biblical slavery was no picnic despite what the liars of the woke church say.

So slavery has existed since ancient times, and the Bible records many examples of the horrors of it in Israel's past. If any nation ever had an excuse to point at their brutal history in order to view their former oppressors with suspicion and partiality, it would be the Israelites. After all, God was literally and objectively on the Israelite's side, and He fully recognized the brutality of the Egyptians. He even punished it severely through the plagues and the angel of death. But God does not let Israelites do this. Rather, His law commands,

> *You must not hate an Egyptian, for you lived as a foreigner in his land.*

The context of this verse is amazing to me. This is not an ishy-squishy, lovey-dovey Bible passage. The Bible is too problematic for that. This verse is not about the all-encompassing inclusivity of the covenant, but rather it is showing the people who must be *excluded* from the assembly of the Lord.

> *A man with crushed or severed genitals may not enter the assembly of the Lord. A person of illegitimate birth may not enter the assembly of the Lord; to the tenth generation no one related to him may do so.*
>
> *No Ammonite or Moabite may enter the assembly of the Lord; to the tenth generation none of their descendants shall ever do so for they did not meet you with food and water on the way as you came from Egypt, and furthermore, they hired Balaam son of Beor of Pethor in Aram Naharaim to curse*

> *you. But the Lord your God refused to listen to Balaam and changed the curse to a blessing, for the Lord your God loves you. You must not seek peace and prosperity for them through all the ages to come. You must not hate an Edomite, for he is your relative; you must not hate an Egyptian, for you lived as a foreigner in his land. Children of the third generation born to them may enter the assembly of the Lord. (Deuteronomy 23:1-8, NET)* [79]

The first thing to note is that God is not telling His people to ignore history. In fact, the entire context is *reminding* the Israelites about their history. Ammonites and Moabites cannot enter the assembly of God for ten generations because of what happened in history. Ten generations of exclusion because of what happened in history! But when God gets to the Egyptians, we get a different story.

Egyptians are only excluded for two generations. The third may enter the assembly of the Lord. God explains that the reason He is allowing this is because Egypt allowed Israel to sojourn in their land. Not only is the amount of exclusion reduced because of this, but also God requires that the Israelite not hate Egyptians. Why do you think God calls out a special command regarding the prohibition of hatred against Egyptians? Why did He not just say, "Don't hate anybody"?

The idea here is that God is addressing and correcting what would likely be the strongest temptation for His people. It's the

---

79 https://www.biblegateway.com/passage/?search=Deuteronomy+23&version=NET

same reason why we don't need a Bible verse that says, "Love your friend." We naturally love our friends. But the temptation is to hate our enemies, so we need to hear God command us to love them. Remember, as we discussed in chapter 2, love is primarily an action, not a feeling. The same is true for hate. You can feel hatred, but first and foremost hatred is expressed in how you treat someone. God's people were to treat Egyptians according to the law of God. In this way, they were to love them.

God knew that based on the history of oppression it would be a massive temptation for Israel to treat Egyptians with partiality. He decided to speak to this issue directly. God reminded the people that "the history," as it were, was not monolithic. There was oppression, yes, but there was also generosity. Israel was enslaved by Egypt, yes, but Israel was not allowed to have selective memory when it came to their history. John Calvin put it this way:

> *Although, therefore, the Israelites had been unworthily oppressed by their fierce tyranny, still God would have their old kindness acknowledged; since their dearth and famine had been relieved, and the refugees were kindly received, when the inhabitants of Canaan were perishing of hunger.*[80]

Before they were slaves they were invited guests in the land of Egypt. Their history was not one dimensional. History rarely is. In fact, when you consider the circumstances around Israel's sojourning in Egypt in the first place, you find the patriarchs

80 https://biblehub.com/commentaries/calvin/deuteronomy/23.htm

themselves acted shamefully. They beat and sold their own brother, Joseph, into Egyptian slavery which set off a chain of events leading to their sojourning and eventual enslavement to Egypt. History is messy like that, and God won't let His people forget it. It is easy to let hatred blind you to the reality about people. Hidden hatred often lies behind lies, half-truths, and partiality.

> *You must not hate an Egyptian, for you lived as a foreigner in his land.*

The proper application of this verse is crucial to the woke church controversy in evangelicalism.

The George Whitefield Controversy

The American reformer George Whitefield has been a central battleground in the woke church controversy in the same way the Confederate flag has in the culture at large. On the one hand, many people celebrate Whitefield as a great theologian, preacher, and brother in the Lord. His writings are remarkable and rich. His insights have been highly valuable to a great many Christians. We have no doubt about this. On the other hand, George Whitefield owned black slaves. He also defended the institution of slavery in general. In an article titled "Was George Whitefield a Christian?" woke evangelical author Jared C. Wilson put the dilemma this way:

> *How can someone who apparently knew the gospel so well not see his own duplicity? Or, perhaps seeing it, not care?*

> *We cannot rightly say this was a "blind spot" in the man's life because of his contrary views previously. How might we wrestle with the tainted legacy of George Whitefield?*[81]

This is a question worth wrestling with. It is a question every believer has dealt with when thinking about themselves. I love Christ, and I trust Him. I know He died on the cross to pay for my sins, and yet I still sin. I don't want to sin, but I do. I resolve in myself never again to return to my sin, but then I do. Why? What do we make of this? Am I even a Christian? Was George Whitefield?

One of my favorite responses to this exact question answers this way:

> *Christ's sacrifice on the cross and resurrection out of the grave are big enough, grand enough, effective enough, and eternal enough to cover your shoddy Christian life.*[82]

This quotation is also from Jared C. Wilson. It is gospel-centered and true. Christians have always confessed that we do not look to ourselves and our works to decide whether we are saved, but rather we look to Christ and His work. This is Christianity 101. Basic gospel. So why is Jared Wilson so hesitant to apply it to George Whitefield?

On the one hand, he does. His article concludes:

81 https://ftc.co/resource-library/blog-entries/was-george-whitefield-a-christian/

82 http://www.christcenteredlife.com/firstchapter.asp?mode=view&index=1386

> *In the end, I hope and trust Whitefield was saved, not because I have benefited from his work (though I have), but because I am sure I will die with sin unrepented of myself, and as the worst sinner I know, my only hope is found not on the grand scale weighing my good against my bad, but on the grand cross of Christ, where even the vilest of sinners may find atonement.*

He seems to land in the right place. Sort of. He *hopes* Christ's sacrifice is big enough, grand enough, effective enough, and eternal enough to cover Whitefield's shoddy Christian life, but he doesn't seem so sure. Earlier in the article he speaks of Christians who do not believe Whitefield was a Christian.

> *First, I have no complaints with those who cannot believe he was.... I especially understand not just how my African-American brothers and sisters cannot answer in the affirmative, but also how they cannot abide white evangelical "whitewashing" his legacy. I cannot feel what they feel, but I can understand why they feel it. I have no interest in diminishing that or chastising that... affirm the rationale of those who answer the question of Whitefield's salvation "no," and I affirm their freedom to do so. I see how you get there. I respect the conclusion. I will not argue it.*

Wilson is not alone in this perspective. This is representative of the general woke church position on Christian slaveholders like George Whitefield. While a small minority believe slaveholding to be the unforgivable sin, most, like Wilson, argue it is not necessarily unforgiveable; but they can understand why some might think it was.

Let me be clear. This is a compromise on the very gospel itself. If a person needs to repent of each sin individually for Christ's sacrifice to work for them, then all is lost. Wilson knows this; yet he is willing to allow the salvation of a Christian, who is not here to defend himself, be called into question over this issue. Why has he shown himself willing to compromise the heart of the gospel message in this way? It is because the woke church has not applied God's warning to Israel correctly. They have hated their version of Egypt.

It is beyond question that Egyptians had mistreated Israelites. We have an infallible record of that mistreatment. Still, God required Israel to treat Egyptians fairly and with love. They were even allowed to be full members of the assembly after two generations. This was a big deal. After two generations of believing Egyptians could join Israel and were no longer "foreigners." They were no longer barred from intermarrying with Israelites after just two generations because, though the Egyptians oppressed His people, they also showed them kindness.

Those who would use different standards to judge George Whitefield's salvation than they would to judge, say, Martin Luther King Jr.'s salvation are doing so because of a hatred toward the Antebellum South. It might be a concealed hatred, but it is a hatred nonetheless. This is why you get nuanced discussions about the salvation of literal, formal heretics, such as Dr. King; but you get suspicion and legalistic standards regarding orthodox Christians who are too connected to the South. This is precisely the thing God warns about in Deuteronomy 23:7. It is the same energy that desires to cancel the Confederate flags and monuments. It's a concealed hatred, based on an ugly history, which God specifically does not allow His people to hold onto.

George Whitefield, like all people, had sin in his life. That being said, we have more evidence of Whitefield's reliance on Christ and His perfect atonement than most any theologian in American history. History is messy and imperfect. We need to recognize this fact.

Jemar Tisby's Abuse of History

Jemar Tisby is one of the most adored evangelical "woke church" celebrities of our time. His books appear on every social justice reading list, and he is a desirable guest on woke podcasts and vlogs. His bestselling book, *The Color of Compromise,* details the American church's ugly history regarding racism. He pulls no punches, and George Whitefield is one of his primary targets.

Tisby's value as a truthful historian is definitely debatable. Still, the history of the American church, in general, and George Whitefield, more specifically, is at best a mixed bag. But Tisby goes a step further. One of the main goals of his book is to attempt to demonstrate that the church in America has a racist history and is still fundamentally racist to this day.

> *Since the 1970s, Christian complicity in racism has become more difficult to discern. It is hidden, but that does not mean it no longer exists. As we look more closely at*

> *the realm of politics, we see that Christian complicity with racism remains, even as it has taken on subtler forms. Again, we must remember; racism never goes away; it adapts... One of the challenges we face in discussions of racism today is that the conversation about race has shifted since the civil rights era. Legislation has rendered the most overt acts of racism legally punishable. Hate crimes of various forms still occur, but most American Christians would call these acts evil. Yet the legacy of racism persists, albeit in different forms.*[83]

This is a remarkable statement. Tisby uses the history of the American church to judge the American church in the present day. This is a direct violation of Deuteronomy 23:7 as well as many other commands from God. Tisby admits no explicit evidence connects the American church in the present to complicity in racism in the present. In an advanced copy of the book, blogger and anti-abortion advocate Samuel Sey quotes Tisby saying this more explicitly:

> *At this point, readers of this book may be wondering if we will find the proverbial "smoking gun"—explicit evidence that connects the American church with overt complicity in racism. While there is no smoking gun here, we must remember that even though racism never goes away, it adapts.*[84]

---

83 Jemar Tisby, *The Color of Compromise: The Truth about the American Church's Complicity in Racism* (Grand Rapids, MI: Zondervan, 2020), chapter 9.

84 https://slowtowrite.com/the-color-of-compromise/

Tisby admits that modern American Christians would condemn hate crimes and other overt acts of racism. Tisby also admits that legislation against racism is supported by American Christians; yet the American church is *still* complicit in racism in his view. Why? To Tisby, modern Christians are still complicit because the American church has a history of racism. Because the American church used to be guilty of racism, according to history, it is still guilty of racism because racism never goes away; it just changes form. How does he know this? He just assumes it. He uses this judgment against the historical American church to push a variety of progressive reforms that fall directly into line with every partisan social justice/woke church political ideal imaginable. As we've seen in part 1, all of these schemes break the law of God. In other words, they are examples of hatred. And,

> *you must not hate an Egyptian, for you lived as a foreigner in his land.*

Nor should you hate a Southerner. Even if you accept the absolute worst version of the historical record (the kind Tisby presents) you still cannot break the law of God regarding the descendants of those Southerners. This was true of Egyptians for Israel, and it is still true for the people of God today. This is especially applicable to those you share fellowship with in Christ. Yes, even though Southern Christians had sin issues we find deplorable in modern times, we are still part of the same assembly. This leads us to the nature of that assembly and the topic of the next chapter.

CHAPTER 8
You Shall Hate Your Father and Mother—Rejecting the Flesh

"If any man come to me, and hate not his father, and mother, and wife, and children, and brethren, and sisters, yea, and his own life also, he cannot be my disciple."

—Luke 14:26

I fully admit I am a bit of a strange person. My favorite Bible verses tend to be the ones most people have trouble with. One day we will talk about how much I love Genesis 1:6-8, but that is for another time. More seriously, I find the verses no one would ever dream of putting on a coffee mug often teach important things about God and what He is like. I love Luke 14:26 for the woke church controversy for two primary reasons.

First, our Lord Himself spoke it. This is advantageous, strategically speaking. All of Scripture is authoritative and God-breathed, but some professing Christians put more weight on the words of Jesus than they do on the Old Testament or the writings of Paul or John. They are known broadly as "red-letter" Christians. "Red-letter" Christians tend to be very woke and social-justice focused. Just a quick perusal of the home page of www.redletterchristians.org will likely produce a variety of social-justice themed articles. "Red-letter Christianity" is not a legitimate approach since it is not what the Bible teaches, nor is it what Jesus Himself taught. Even so, it can be helpful to have verses directly from the mouth of Jesus that refute the basic foundations of the woke church. Woke church advocates have a much more difficult time waving away statements from Jesus than they do from God's holy law.

Second, the forceful language used here is hard to miss. Jesus intentionally uses very strong language to get His point across. It is impossible to gloss over this statement without taking notice. Hate? Jesus, really? Does He not know that love trumps hate? What is He doing? Jesus' words here smack you in the mouth, and it becomes impossible not to pay attention. It grates on the sensibilities of all the standard evangelical approaches to theology that I can imagine. I love it.

Racial Idolatry

The woke church is profoundly obsessed with skin color. Skin color explains literally everything in their system. If you can find a disparity anywhere, then skin color can explain it. Skin color drives gaps in income, wealth, insurance rates, health outcomes, property ownership, access to hiking trails, the disparity in Magic: The Gathering participation rates and many others. For a great example of this kind of ridiculously simplistic thinking, take a look at Phil Vischer's YouTube video, "Race in America."

But even beyond simply disparities, skin color also determines the difference between good actions and evil actions in the woke church system. If you want to make something sound extra evil, add the modifier "white" to the beginning. "White" fragility is the evil kind of fragility. It's way worse than the neutral, passive kind of fragile. "White" tears are the kind of tears that demons shed when they are trying to manipulate you. "White" silence is the violent kind of silence, and don't even get me started on the kind of gaze a "white" gaze is. I dare you to do internet searches on some of these terms from professed Christian sources. It may be enough to scare anyone straight.

On the other hand, if you desire to make something sound noble and pure, add "black" to the beginning. "Black" forgiveness is the purest kind of forgiveness in existence. "Black" excellence is like regular excellence, except more excellent. Even things that normally would be a negative can be made positive by adding "black" to it. Search online for "black rage." Dante Stewart, a mainstream woke church leader, has written some strange articles on the virtue of this kind of fury.

According to the woke church movement, skin color plays a fundamentally important role when considering a person's community and identity. Thabiti Anyabwile, a woke church leader and pastor, in a revealing twitter thread, put the dilemma he sees for black-skinned professing Christians like this. It is a long quotation, but it will reveal the true danger of this mindset thoroughly.

> *There's something I've been trying to find words to express for some time. I'm still not confident these are the words, but I will use them and ask you, dear reader, to receive them as best as God's grace will allow you. I'm still grappling for better expression. I am grateful for the many white brethren in Christ who have expressed genuine concern and weariness about recent events. I appreciate the expressions, and, like many, I draw some encouragement from them. Please don't stop sharing how you feel. A lot of the expressions of empathy are addressed to African Americans as "brothers and sisters in Christ." A welcome that recognition of our kinship in the Lord—especially when a number of other professing Christians weaponize and politicize that kinship to deny justice. But it must be said—and here's where I struggle to find the correct words—that the site of our struggle is NOT our shared Christian faith. Therefore expressing *Christian* solidarity falls short of the kind of solidarity that's needed in the moment. To put it another way: George Floyd--a Christian, as I understand it--was NOT mistreated and killed because he was a Christian. Breonna Taylor was not killed because she was a Christian. Same for Ahmaud Arberry [sic]. The man in Central Park was not threatened b/c he was a Christian. They were killed or threatened because of the country's attitude toward Black people. The site of the struggle*

*is anti-black sentiment, discrimination, and injustice. Therefore, the solidarity *most* needed is with *Black people as a people--Christian or not.* I know some people from various ethnic backgrounds are attempting to express precisely that solidarity with Black people as Black people. I am grateful for that. But I want Christian brethren to realize that emphasizing Christian solidarity misconstrues the struggle. More, misconstruing the struggle in this way forces a terrible choice upon Black Christians—do we embrace Christian solidarity to the detriment of Black existence/struggle, or do we emphasize Black survival/flourishing to the detriment of Christian solidarity? This is a real world dynamic for many Black Christians. It's not that we don't understand unity in Christ. It's that we cannot afford to underline that unity when the threat is against Black people whether or not they're Christians. The extension of empathy only along Christian lines and with the tacit expectation that we define ourselves solely in terms of our Christian identity, is ultimately a self-destructive proposition for the Black Christian. We cannot accept such terms and survive. On the other hand, the rejection of Christian solidarity in order to emphasize Black survival and well-being causes consternation for those of us who deeply believe in the gospel's reconciling power. Both options are a kind of suicide of something vitally important. What's needed is: 1. Solidarity with us *as Black people.* 2. Your emphasizing solidarity with Black people to such an extent that we're in turn freed to accept and emphasize solidarity in Christ. Until that happens, we'll have to choose*

> *Black solidarity b4 Xian to live. I want you to be in the fight with us. But you need to be in the fight *on the right basis.* You'll need to understand how the current issues effect us *as Black people* and not as Christian people. Until you understand that, you'll distract from the focus that's needed. Again, I'm trusting your charitable reading, and I'm grateful for your expressions of empathy. Stand with Black people as a people because we're facing injustices as Black people not as Christians. I hope that's helpful in some way.*[85]

As a Christian, you are someone who bears the name of Christ. This is what the word "Christian" means. Revelation 22:4 says that His name is written on our heads. This means we are identified with Him. The Bible also speaks of the assembly, the church, as Christ's own body. We are identified with Him. The Scriptures again and again emphasis the union Christians have with Christ and in Christ. This is a matter of first importance. John Calvin elaborates:

> *I confess that we are deprived of this utterly incomparable good until Christ is made ours. Therefore, that joining of Head and members, that indwelling of Christ in our hearts—in short, that mystical union—are accorded by us the highest degree of importance, so that Christ, having been made ours, makes us sharers with him in the gifts with which he has been endowed. We do not, therefore, contemplate him outside ourselves from afar in order that his righteousness may be*

85 https://twitter.com/thabitianyabwil/status/1266794880581488642?lang=en

> *imputed to us but because we put on Christ and are engrafted into his body—in short, because he deigns to make us one with him. For this reason, we glory that we have fellowship of righteousness with him.*[86]

In short, without our union and identity in Christ we have no Christian religion. This is basic. We come together for Christ and because of Christ. Our identity in Christ is of first importance. This is nonnegotiable for a Christian. But not to the woke church. According to Anyabwile, and the woke church, in general, the Christian identity can be a liability.

Another reason I provided the long quotation from Anyabwile above is because I doubt you would believe me if I just attempted to summarize it. Read it again, just so it is fresh in your mind. It is hard to imagine anyone bearing the name of Christ could honestly think this way.

Anyabwile wrote the thread above due to a sincere concern about fellow Christians addressing their words of encouragement to black friends as "brothers and sisters in Christ." (Horror, I know.) To Anyabwile, while this is not a bad thing in itself, it is not the kind of "kinship" or communion that is needed right now. Rather, what is more important is not that you identify together with Christ, but that you identify with black people's black skin. This is the kinship and identity that is needed, even "to the detriment of Christianity solidarity"! Anyabwile goes so far as to say that to identify primarily in Christ is a suicidal proposition for black people. And that if given the choice between identifying

86 John Calvin, *Institutes of the Christian Religion*. 3.11.10, pp. 736-37.

with black skin or identifying in Christ, black people must choose identifying with black skin in order to live.

I don't think I have to convince you of this fact, but the above paragraph, if true, would be the end of the Christian faith. It is idolatry of the highest order. It is the very definition of "living in the flesh," and it is the exact kind of thing that Christ, in Luke 14:26, says makes someone "not able to be His disciple." One thing to keep in mind is that Anyabwile, and many in the woke church movement, are addressing people they consider allies. This is not addressed to fake Christians or racist Christians. This is addressed to woke white Christians who already agree with them about the highly debatable race narratives in our country, and *still* he will not choose Christian identity with them over black skin identity. This is the most overtly carnal belief I can imagine a Christian believing. It is pagan idolatry.

Hate Your Mother and Father

So what did Jesus mean when He said you cannot be His disciple unless you hate your father and mother and even your own life? Surely Jesus could not have been contradicting the law of God. The first commandment with a promise says, "Honor your father and your mother." A Christian is committed to the idea that all of Scripture is God's Word and infallible. Contradiction is not an option. As usual, the context of Jesus' statement makes the meaning clear. Jesus is talking about loyalty.

The surrounding verses of Luke 14 show that Jesus wants people to know what they are getting themselves into if they decide to follow Him. This is not a minor association or a part-time club to join. Jesus requires complete and total devotion from His followers. Of course He requires this. Jesus is God in flesh. We shall have no other gods before Him.

This means that when it comes to loyalty and devotion the natural human instinct for loyalty toward your own family must come after your loyalty to Christ. You must love Christ with everything you have. You must love Christ more than your own flesh and blood. Your love for Christ must make your love for your own family look like hatred in comparison. It must be a total love. But, as we've established, love is primarily an action, not a feeling. So to love Christ means to obey Him in everything. Every command Christ gives to His people must be regarded and obeyed completely without regard for the considerations and desires of others. This includes the desire of your own flesh and blood.

This works itself out in the life of a Christian every day. For an easy example, consider that as a husband and father God requires me to love my wife and children. This means I am to provide for their needs including shelter, clothing, and food. This is a command straight from God that happens to be something many men find quite natural to do. Suppose I found myself in poverty and was unable to provide for my family through legitimate means; but I found a situation where I could steal from someone in order to make an income in order to provide for my family. Say it was a rich person that would never even notice they had been stolen from. What should I do? As a Christian I must not provide for my family in that way. This is because God has told His people that we shall not steal. To an outsider my devotion to God and His commandments may look like neglecting the needs of my family.

It may look as if I hate them since I could easily just steal and provide for them. But for a Christian the order of operations must start with Christ and His commands. Our devotion to Him must be total. This is what Luke 14:26 is all about.

John Calvin wrote:

> *Let the husband then love his wife, the father his son, and, on the other hand, let the son love his father, provided that the reverence which is due to Christ be not overpowered by human affection. For if even among men, in proportion to the closeness of the tie that mutually binds us, some have stronger claims than others, it is shameful that all should not be deemed inferior to Christ alone. And certainly we do not consider sufficiently, or with due gratitude, what it is to be a disciple of Christ, if the excellence of this rank be not sufficient to subdue all the affections of the flesh.*[87]

Notice what is not being said. It is not the case that natural human affections for your family are illegitimate or wrong. On the contrary, the fact that Jesus uses such intentionally harsh and jarring language about these affections, in comparison to how we should love Him, actually affirms the rightness and goodness of the affections themselves. I do not believe that seeking good things for the people of your ethnicity is a bad thing. The dividing line is that we must prioritize God's commands before we even consider the needs and desires of our families, especially our extended

87 https://biblehub.com/commentaries/calvin/luke/14.htm

families according to ethnicity. God and His commands always come first.

The woke church is guilty of loving their extended family according to the flesh more than Christ. Thabiti Anyabwile's comments make this crystal clear. If given the choice between identifying with his ethnic family according to skin color and identifying with Christians according to the fellowship of the Holy Spirit, Anyabwile chooses ethnicity. To him, this is a choice between life and death. Identifying with his brothers in the flesh is "Black survival." He has decided "*to choose Black solidarity b4 Xian to live.*"

I do not for a second grant to Thabiti Anyabwile that this really is a choice between life and death. I think this is an objectively false statement and an attempt to be overly dramatic. But, for argument's sake, let's say it really was this serious. Let's say choosing to identify with black skin meant saving your life, while choosing to identify with American Christians was a type of "suicide," as he says. Would it be okay to choose black identity over Christian?

This may seem reasonable to some people, but it is a direct contradiction to Jesus' commands. Choosing life through disloyalty or disobedience to Him is not an option for a disciple of Jesus Christ. In his commentary John Calvin cross references Luke 14:26 with a similar passage from Matthew 10. Here is the relevant passage.

> *Do not think that I have come to bring peace to the earth. I have not come to bring peace, but a sword. For I have come*

> *to set a man against his father, and a daughter against her mother, and a daughter-in-law against her mother-in-law. And a person's enemies will be those of his own household. Whoever loves father or mother more than me is not worthy of me, and whoever loves son or daughter more than me is not worthy of me. And whoever does not take his cross and follow me is not worthy of me. Whoever finds his life will lose it, and whoever loses his life for my sake will find it. (Matthew 10:34-39, ESV)*[88]

Jesus' call is a call to complete devotion. We dare not disobey our Lord no matter what the cost is according to the flesh, even if that cost is death. It is a very good thing to have love for your family and even your ethnicity in general. (After all, what is ethnicity but an extended family?) But this love must be subordinate to the way a Christian loves Christ and His people. That is, love of God is foundational. Love for others flows from the love of God. We must never bend the rules, show partiality, or flat out break the commandments of God in an attempt to love others. It never works that way. That is a counterfeit version of love. That is idolatry. Our devotion and loyalty to Christ must make our love for our brothers according to the flesh look like hatred by comparison, even if it costs us our lives.

88 https://www.biblegateway.com/passage/?search=Matthew%2010&version=ESV

CHAPTER 9
Debt and Forgiveness—The Missing Piece of Woke Theology

"So likewise shall my heavenly Father do also unto you, if ye from your hearts forgive not every one his brother their trespasses."
—Matthew 18:35

If you ask any Christian what is so great about Jesus, the topic of forgiveness will likely come up. Christians often say we are not better *people* than unbelievers, but we are *better off* than they are. This is because of the power of forgiveness. The Bible says the "blessed man" is the man whose sin God does not hold against him. This is only possible due to forgiveness. Forgiveness is wonderful. It is why we come together and sing to Christ every Sunday. Forgiveness is central to our faith in Christ.

But, in many ways, forgiveness does not come naturally to us without divine intervention. It often seems like a concept that we literally need a miracle worked within us to truly understand. Everybody wants to be forgiven their own debts—that part comes naturally. Where it gets skewed is when it comes to forgiving others their debts. Jesus knew this, so He taught often on the topic of forgiving others.

Religious people do not typically reject the notion of forgiveness completely. Instead, they try to skew it in their favor. Smaller distortions of forgiveness are what Jesus typically dealt with refuting. In Matthew 18, Peter asked Jesus how many times he needed to forgive someone who wronged him. Peter wasn't rejecting forgiveness per se; he knew he had to forgive. Rather, he was certain there had to be a cut-off point for the amount of forgiveness required. Surely we need not be naïvely forgiving someone for every wrong they commit; there had to be a limit. Jesus' answer was easy to understand and direct.

Jesus saith unto him, I say not unto thee, Until seven times: but, Until seventy times seven.[89]

In other words, no, there was no limit.

Like many of us, Peter often needed a little bit more convincing to understand the lesson fully. To drive the point home Jesus tells a parable about the kingdom of God. The parable is about a servant who owed a great debt to his master. The debt was so large he could not hope to pay it off, and so he simply begged for mercy. Instead of selling the servant and his family, as he originally planned, the master decides not only to give the

89 https://www.biblegateway.com/passage/?search=Matthew+18&version=KJV

servant more time, but to cancel the debt completely. What an amazing gift! The story continues with this same servant coming upon a fellow servant who owed him a much smaller debt. He insisted the man pay and refused to show him mercy as he had been shown. When the master hears of this he is furious. The text reads:

> *"Evil slave! I forgave you all that debt because you begged me! Should you not have shown mercy to your fellow slave, just as I showed it to you?" And in anger his lord turned him over to the prison guards to torture him until he repaid all he owed. So also my heavenly Father will do to you, if each of you does not forgive your brother from your heart. (Matthew 18:32-35, NET)*[90]

Jesus teaches this concept in many places. When His disciples ask Him to teach them how to pray, He gives them a short pattern to follow. Included in this five-sentence-long prayer is,

> *And forgive us our debts, as we forgive our debtors.*

He then summarizes the thrust of the whole short prayer like this:

> *For if ye forgive men their trespasses, your heavenly Father will also forgive you: But if ye forgive not men their trespasses, neither will your Father forgive your trespasses.*

---

90 https://www.biblegateway.com/passage/?search=Matthew+18&version=NET

Forgiveness is central to the Christian faith. God takes this seriously. The Lord told His people we should pray to God that He forgive us as we forgive others. This means that if we want God to forgive us of our sin debt we'd better forgive the sins and debts we have against each other. The idea of an unforgiving Christian makes no sense. A Christian, by definition, cannot be one to withhold forgiveness. We have no right to claim the name of Christ, as one whom God has forgiven, if we do not forgive others. The parable of the unforgiving servant has a message that can be understood by even a small child. If you do not forgive your brother in your heart you are an unbeliever. This concept could not be more clearly taught in the Bible.

So, of course, the woke church movement messes up the concept of forgiveness as well.

If you were one of the few who watched my earliest video content and podcasts you may have noticed a shift in tone over time. I used to be way less hardcore. For the most part, I assumed most of the woke church advocates I followed were real believers who simply had some bad ideas. I refuted the ideas the best I could; but I always bent over backward to talk about the great value each person brought to the Christian community, in general, outside of the bad ideas. That all changed in the fall of 2019. Something happened that year that forced me to face the reality that not everyone I was dealing with was a believer in Christ.

Ironically, the thing that happened was an objectively beautiful courtroom moment. In October 2019 Amber Guyger, a white police officer, was found guilty of murdering a black man named Botham Jean in his home in 2018. The man's brother was a Christian named Brandt. Brandt decided to speak to the court on the day of Amber's sentencing. His words were full of grace and forgiveness for his brother's killer.

> *"If you are truly sorry, I know I can speak for myself, I forgive you."*

He added,

> *"I think giving your life to Christ would be the best thing that Botham would want for you."*

Brandt then spoke to the judge and requested that Amber not be sentenced to jail for her crime. He also asked the judge if he could hug his brother's killer, which the judge granted.

The moment was full of the love of Christ. It was beautiful. The image was shared and marveled at across all forms of media. Many were driven to tears at the forgiveness offered to this woman. It was an amazing testimony to the power of Christ in the heart of a man. Clearly, Brandt had heard the words of Christ from Matthew 18. He had heard them and taken them to heart the way all Christians should.

But not everyone was happy with this display of forgiveness and grace. Woke church advocates everywhere started wringing their hands at the event. Jemar Tisby submitted an opinion piece to the *Washington Post*, which they were all too happy to publish. In an article addressed to white Christians, Tisby lamented the situation.

From a certain perspective, Brandt is simply following the dictates of his conscience and his faith. But what must be understood is that when tragedies such as the murder of a black man by a white police officer occur, they aren't just felt by one black person. The black community feels the impact.[91]

He continues:

Black grief is a community project. It is felt widely but dealt with individually. Some go to therapy. Some participate in demonstrations. Others write op-eds. Everyone is entitled to their own process… No one should expect swift mercy from every black person. And the risk of offering such speedy forgiveness is that not nearly enough attention is given to the injustice itself.

To Tisby, forgiveness is not necessarily the only legitimate Christian response to a repentant person. It's too risky to the black community at large to speedily forgive white people of their sins and crimes. The Lord says,

For if ye forgive men their trespasses, your heavenly Father will also forgive you.

But Tisby says,

91 https://www.washingtonpost.com/religion/2019/10/03/white-christians-do-not-cheapen-hug-message-forgiveness-botham-jeans-brother/

Instant absolution minimizes the magnitude of injustice.

Jesus warns,

So also my heavenly Father will do to you, if each of you does not forgive your brother from your heart.

Tisby warns,

*No one should mistake black forgiveness, whenever and **if ever** it is offered, for complacency with racial injustice.* (emphasis added)

Tisby is not alone in twisting the basic concept of Christian forgiveness for the woke church. In an article called "You Don't Have to Accept the Sorry," professing Christian Heather Day explains how she teaches her children that forgiveness is actually more about you and your own feelings than it is about duty to God.

I don't want my daughter to think that forgiveness is a burden someone else can put on her. I want her to grow up feeling worthy of time and space. We don't get to choose how or when people hurt us, but we do get to choose how and when we are ready to forgive them. Forgiveness is not for them. Forgiveness is for us.[92]

92 https://faithfullymagazine.com/dont-accept-sorry/

I provide the citation for this quote, but I can save you time if you were going to look and see if a Bible verse was referenced for this teaching. The answer is no, there isn't.

The concept of withholding forgiveness is nothing new for the social justice movement in the church. Jemar Tisby did not come up with these ideas out of nowhere. Rather he learned them from his favorite theologian, James Cone.

James Cone—The Godfather of the Woke Church

James Cone was a black liberation theologian who passed away in 2018. When he died, Jemar Tisby and many other woke church leaders waxed poetic about how much they owe to Cone's writings for their own ideas and beliefs. James Cone was a literal, capital "H" heretic. He denied every single one of the fundamentals of the faith. An abject lack of forgiveness as a priority was a big part of that. In his highly acclaimed book outlining the basics of his heretical faith, he spoke about the situation for blacks in America in the 1960s.

> *White appeals to "wait and talk it over" are irrelevant when children are dying and men and women are being tortured. We will not let whitey cool this one with his pious love ethic but will seek to enhance our hostility bringing it to its full manifestation....*[93]

---

93 James Cone, *A Black Theology of Liberation* (Philadelphia, PA: J.B. Lippincott Company, 1970), p. 35.

In the next section, Cone describes in more detail what this hostility includes.

> *We have reached our limit of tolerance, and if it means death with dignity, or life with humiliation, we will choose the former. And if that is the choice, we will take some honkies with us.*[94]

At this point you may be wondering why the crown jewel of woke theological thought sounds like he is more interested in revenge than he is forgiveness. James has a succinct answer to that.

> *Black Theology refuses to accept a God who is not identified totally with the goals of the black community.*[95]

This means any theological idea that is not advantageous to blacks and their interests can be rejected, even if it seems to be taught in the pages of the Bible. Does Christ say to "love your enemy"? Well, that must be the "white" Christ speaking, since Black Theology would teach that loving your oppressor is a sin.

> *Their sin is that of trying to "understand" the enslaver, to "love" him on his own terms. As the oppressed community recognize their situation in the light of God's revelation, they know now that they should have killed him instead of loving him.*[96]

94 Ibid., p. 42.
95 Ibid., p. 59.
96 Ibid., p. 101.

James Cone spoke prophetically to our times as well. Ever wonder why the woke church downplays modern race riots? They didn't invent this; they got it from their favorite theologian. "Black Christ" affirms such things.

> *To be a disciple of the Black Christ is to become black with him. Looting, burning, or the so-called "destruction" of white property are not primary concerns. Such matters can only be decided by the oppressed themselves who are seeking to develop their images of the Black Christ.*[97]

You say, "How can this be? This is not how Christ taught and behaved. Is not Christ the example for those who bear His name to follow?" You foolish white fundamentalist,

> *We cannot use Jesus' behavior in the first century as a literal guide for our actions in the twentieth century. To do so is to fall into the same trap that the fundamentalists are guilty of. It destroys the freedom of the Christian man, the freedom to make decisions without an ethical guide from Jesus.*[98]

Still cannot accept it? Maybe you follow the "White Christ." Don't worry. He is on the list too.

> *What need have we for a white Christ when we are not white but black? If Christ is white and not black, he is an oppressor, and we must kill him.*[99]

---

97 Ibid., p. 219.
98 Ibid., p. 68.
99 Ibid., p. 199.

Trust me when I tell you that you can find equally mad ravings of the lunatic that was James Cone on almost every single page of his writing. It is no wonder forgiveness is downplayed in the woke church movement even as it is a primary focus in the Bible. Their teachers were flat out heretics and probably clinically insane. Of course, modern woke church theologians have a "nicer" way of putting it, but what difference does that make? We are talking about the same thing whether it is dressed in flowery subversive language or direct speech, as in Cone. Frankly, I prefer confronting heresy that is straight up.

I was once quoted as a "token" conservative in a *New York Times* article on the social justice controversy in the church. The author of the article was quite sympathetic to the woke church, but even she was able to identify the radical nature of the influence James Cone's heretical beliefs have had on the movement.

> *Radical thinkers have found their way into the citadels of white evangelicalism. Reading the black liberation theologian James Cone helped Mr. Strickland, the theology professor, see how white theologians often ignore the structural sources of earthly suffering.*[100]

Professor Walter Strickland is an evangelical favorite. Teaching at a flagship Southern Baptist seminary he admitted his clandestine approach to the *New York Times* reporter.

---

100 https://www.nytimes.com/2019/04/20/opinion/sunday/black-evangelicals-diversity.html

When he speaks to conservative white congregations, he is careful: "While Cone's ideas are in play, I don't mention him by name, because I don't want to put unnecessary stumbling blocks in their way."

Stumbling blocks, indeed.

Still, the woke church emphasizes something that is not only correct, but also very important to keep in mind about the concept of forgiveness. We must avoid an overly narrow biblical message that emphasizes forgiveness but neglects righteousness. We must be about both since the Bible is about both.

Evangelicals often call the cross of Christ "the place where mercy and justice meet." This is correct. Since God is completely holy, He must justly punish sin. Since God shows His people mercy, He also wants to forgive sin. By Christ taking the sins of His people upon Himself and enduring the wrath of God against sin Himself, justice is done and mercy is given. So while forgiveness is central, necessary and required for Christians, we must not ignore issues of justice.

Woke church darling Matt Chandler lamented this problem in a virtual sermon delivered in 2020. Visibly frustrated at Christian responses to the riots and looting perpetrated by "Black Lives Matter" supporters (remember this is straight out of James Cone's theology), he shouted at his virtual audience regarding what he called a "brain broke disjoint."[101]

---

101 For a more complete treatment on Matt Chandler's thoughts on this topic please watch my video "A Reasonable Latino Calmly Responds to Matt Chandler," https://www.youtube.com/watch?v=m55gbHMEZAg

> *You don't just "preach the gospel" to sex trafficking! You don't just "preach the gospel" on the issue of life and abortion! No! You act!*

And Matt is exactly right. Sex traffickers should be preached to, and it is hoped they repent and are forgiven for their sins. But their crimes still ought to be punished according to Scripture. This is a death penalty offense. Likewise abortionists and women who kill their children. They need the gospel to save them from their sins. But their crimes are serious, and justice must be done. Most abortions should be tried and punished as capitol murder. All of these issues must use Scripture as the standard for what to do.

And the Scripture says forgiveness is not optional for a Christian, not even a black one. For a Christian, there should be no "if" when it comes to the topic of forgiveness. But, likewise, justice is not optional for a Christian. There is no "if" when it comes to whether justice should be done. It always should be done.

As I have argued throughout this book, we must always use the Bible as the standard for these kinds of things. God tells His people how to act in particular situations. We must be completely sold out to His Word whether the topic is justice or forgiveness. We dare not act as if the Bible does not address these things clearly and completely when it does. If we can be sure about any teaching from the Bible we can be sure of this—if a man claims to know Christ but bristles at forgiveness and downplays its significance in his life, he lies. He does not know Christ, and Christ does not know him. How can someone truly understand the massive weight of sin that was forgiven them by Christ, yet withhold forgiveness for the comparatively much smaller debt their fellow servant owes them? Jesus' answer is clear. He can't.

CHAPTER 10

Every Tribe, Language, and Nation—God's Providence

"And they sang a new song, saying, "Worthy are you to take the scroll and to open its seals, for you were slain, and by your blood you ransomed people for God from every tribe and language and people and nation."

—Revelation 5:9, ESV

Revelation 5:9 contains one of the single most popular phrases used by the woke church movement—"every tribe, language, and nation." Pick any woke evangelical leader and search this phrase. You will find it is referenced in sermons and speeches, used in blog posts, and tweeted out with frequency. The focus of these references is almost always the ethnic diversity of the multitude of people worshipping God. Woke rapper Shai Linne, in an article for *The Gospel Coalition*, recommends teaching your children early about the glories of ethnic diversity.

> *Ethnic diversity isn't something that should be begrudgingly tolerated, but enthusiastically celebrated. Passages like Revelation 5:9-10 speak loudly to God's ultimate purpose in the gospel—a redeemed, ethnically diverse people worshiping him together for all eternity.*[102]

Linne argues that ethnic diversity is not only God's purpose in eternity, but it should be our purpose here and now as well.

> *And we must stress that the goal of multiethnic worship isn't only for heaven; we must pursue it now.*

I see no reason to disagree with Shai Linne about this at a basic level. Revelation 5:9 and other passages that use the "every tribe, language, and nation" phrase are verses that every Christian should hold onto dearly, especially if you are concerned with the growth of the woke church. As we will see, I believe this verse actually works against core aspects of the woke church's project. Also, most Christians should love this verse since, if not for what these verses teach, many of us would not even be in the kingdom of God.

The Bible was written in a specific context by specific authors to a specific audience. Good students will always keep this in mind

102 https://www.thegospelcoalition.org/article/child-ethnic-diversity/

when trying to interpret a Bible verse. A large chunk of the Bible was written by Israelites, to Israelites. This is not debatable. So when we read about "every tribe, language, and nation" we need to figure out what the original audience would have understood this to be referring to by keeping in mind the original author and the original audience.

The Bible speaks of "the nations" often. In fact, in the article referenced, Shai Linne offers a decent list of passages where the Bible speaks this way. From Genesis 17:4 through Daniel 7:14 to the book of Revelation, God's concern for and claim over "the nations" is mentioned everywhere. The identity of "the nations" is crystal clear in the Bible. Theologian Matthew Henry explains the use of the phrase in Revelation.

> *Though these are not said to be sealed, yet they were selected by God out of all nations, and brought into his church, and there stood before the throne. Observe, [1.] God will have a greater harvest of souls among the Gentiles than he had among the Jews. More are the children of the desolate than of the married woman. [2.] The Lord knows who are his, and he will keep them safe in times of dangerous temptation. [3.] Though the church of God is but a little flock, in comparison of the wicked world, yet it is no contemptible society, but really large and to be still more enlarged...The praises offered up by the saints (and, as it seems to me, by the Gentile believers) for the care of God in reserving so large a remnant of the Jews, and saving them from infidelity and destruction. The Jewish church prayed for the Gentiles before their conversion,*

> *and the Gentile churches have reason to bless God for his distinguishing mercy to so many of the Jews, when the rest were cut off.*[103]

When John references every tribe, language, and nation he is clearly referring to a multitude of Gentile believers joining the people of God in worship. Had God's plan not been to include multitudes of Gentiles in His kingdom most of the people reading this book, myself included, would be left on the outside looking in.

Paul the apostle, the very first Christian genius, drives this point home in his letter to the church at Rome. He writes to his primarily Jewish audience:

> *Then what becomes of our boasting? It is excluded. By what kind of law? By a law of works? No, but by the law of faith. For we hold that one is justified by faith apart from works of the law. Or is God the God of Jews only? Is he not the God of Gentiles also? Yes, of Gentiles also, since God is one—who will justify the circumcised by faith and the uncircumcised through faith. Do we then overthrow the law by this faith? By no means! On the contrary, we uphold the law.(Romans 3:27-31, ESV)*[104]

A few sentences later, Paul even references "the nations" in regard to the promise made to Abraham, all the way back in the book of Genesis.

---

103 https://www.christianity.com/bible/commentary.php?com=mh&b=66&c=7
104 https://www.biblegateway.com/passage/?search=Romans%203&version=ESV

As it is written, "I have made you the father of many nations"—in the presence of the God in whom he believed, who gives life to the dead and calls into existence the things that do not exist. In hope he believed against hope, that he should become the father of many nations, as he had been told, "So shall your offspring be.(Romans 4:17-18, ESV)"[105]

The point here is that God's plan for all the nations to worship Him has been in place since the beginning. This is not a new revelation in Revelation. When John's original audience read his book they would have had in mind the promise made to Abraham in the beginning. They would have thought about Daniel's prophecy in Daniel 7:14 referencing the kingdom made up of all the nations. They would have remembered Paul's teaching about God being the God of the Gentiles also. They would have remembered all of these things as they read Revelation 5:9, and they would have seen the promises of God fulfilled. God's faithfulness to His promises would have been the focus. The focus of this passage, like every passage in the Bible, is the truth about what God is like.

If there was ever a passage in the Bible that was focused on Christ, and not people, it would be this one. Everything in the scene is emphasizing the supremacy of Christ. Angels are worshipping. The nations are worshipping. Christ has shown himself faithful to the end, and He is receiving great glory and honor and praise for His work.

Those of us who oppose the distortions of the woke church must not allow them to twist the emphasis of this verse. This belongs

105 https://www.biblegateway.com/passage/?search=Romans%204&version=ESV

to the true church. The scene here is one of total assimilation to Christ's kingdom. The church of God is a church of colonizers. God's kingdom is unique and good. The nations are welcome to join in, but only after they surrender to God completely. Notice what is happening around Christ's throne.

First, the nations are coming together to sing the same song. It's a new song, and it's about the mighty works of God.

> *Worthy are you to take the scroll and to open its seals, for you were slain, and by your blood you ransomed people for God from every tribe and language and people and nation.*

The nations must put away all of their idols. The nations do not come to the throne on their own terms. They may only come on God's terms. This means the kingdom of God is a new culture. It is a Christian culture. There is no neutrality when it comes to the practices and traditions of the nations. Every people group, of every color and ethnicity, must be conformed to the culture of the kingdom of God completely. This is a nonnegotiable, and this is made clear by the passage in Revelation.

Revelation 7 uses the same phrase of "every tribe, language, and nation."

> *After this I looked, and behold, a great multitude that no one could number, from every nation, from all tribes and peoples and languages, standing before the throne and before the Lamb, clothed in white robes, with palm branches in their hands, and crying out with a loud voice, "Salvation belongs*

> *to our God who sits on the throne, and to the Lamb!" And all the angels were standing around the throne and around the elders and the four living creatures, and they fell on their faces before the throne and worshiped God, saying, "Amen! Blessing and glory and wisdom and thanksgiving and honor and power and might be to our God forever and ever! Amen. (Revelation 7:9-12, ESV)"*[106]

Notice again the emphasis is on Christ, not the people. But the people, though they are from every nation, are all dressed the same and worshipping the same. There are not many paths to God, nor are there many interpretations of God's Word. They have surrendered to Christ and His kingdom and now worship Christ in one accord. This is a beautiful scene. It highlights many truths about our God and His works. He is the God of the Jews, yes, but the Gentiles also. The Gentiles, having put away every false way, have come to the throne to worship God according to His Word. As with everything, the Word of God is the standard. The nations must be discipled to obey everything their Lord, the Christ, has commanded. This is a call to surrender, and so we must use this passage to call the woke church advocates to do exactly that.

I have seen this passage from Revelation used to attempt to prove all kinds of things. Here is a list of some things you may have heard about Revelation 5:9 and 7:9:

- It proves you need to learn about non-white cultures.
- It proves you need to have more non-white friends.

106 https://www.biblegateway.com/passage/?search=Revelation+7&version=ESV

- It proves our local churches need to have ethnic diversity proportional to our surrounding neighborhood.
- It proves we need ethnic music in our local worship services.
- It proves we need to consider our local church culture to accommodate ethnic norms such as commitment to punctuality, service times, etc.
- It proves we need to have ethnically diverse elders and deacons in our local churches.

Missing from the list is the only application I think makes sense. How can our assembly, regardless of ethnic makeup, become *more faithful* to how the Scripture commands us to operate? The nations in Revelation had come together to do the same thing—worship Christ. They came according to His commands and His desires. The emphasis is on Christ and not the ethnic/cultural desires of the multitudes. The Christian culture is a distinct culture. It has its own Lord and its own law. All of this is detailed in the book. The woke church makes a priority of emphasizing the cultural distinctives of the nations which is why they get this passage all wrong. I know this idea is overused in evangelicalism, but here it is actually true. This passage is not about you. This is about the King of kings and His rule and reign. We must submit to everything Christ commands. The passage is not about the cultural distinctives of the nations. It is focused completely on the Lamb of God and the kingdom He rules. We all must assimilate to it unconditionally.

One thing that is regularly missed in woke presentations on Revelation is the fact that we do not engineer ethnic diversity in God's kingdom through quotas, affirmative action, installing hip-hop in our services, or any other scheme like that. The Scripture gives us but one tool in order to accomplish this end—the preaching of the gospel of Jesus Christ. Christ will have a new nation made up of people from all the nations. This is true. But He will have it according to His will and through His methods. We cannot rig the systems through clever schemes. Revelation 5:9 is not a license to try out racially motivated, attractional church models. Revelation 5:9 is not an allowance to bend the ten commandments if you think it will reap a more ethnically diverse harvest. On the contrary, Revelation 5:9 is a glimpse at a fulfilled promise. Christ will build His church through the ordinary means of preaching the gospel, baptizing the nations, and teaching them to observe all of Christ's commands. This means all cultural norms that go against those commands must be demolished and left behind and everyone must assimilate completely into the kingdom of God.

Revelation 5:9 is abused by the woke church in almost every single presentation, but this verse is the *least* woke verse in the entire Bible.

We must make the woke church deal with it.

Conclusion

It's time for a confession. I initially marketed this book as a primer on how you could learn to defeat the woke church movement. The truth is, you can't. Neither can I. At least not on our own. The tactics and arguments part 1 confronted and defeated and the Bible verses we learned in part 2 are all excellent ways to engage the primary issues the woke church brings to the controversy. But it's not enough. Over the years I have been addressing this issue on my YouTube channel and podcast I've learned firsthand that this is first and foremost a spiritual battle that requires spiritual solutions. Pharisees cannot be won solely by facts and logic. Christ maneuvered in his confrontations with the Pharisees with perfection. It only drove them further into their rebellion. As Christ told Nicodemus the Pharisee, it is the Holy Spirit who decides when and where to bring a man into new life.

> *Marvel not that I said unto thee, Ye must be born again. The wind bloweth where it listeth, and thou hearest the sound thereof, but canst not tell whence it cometh, and whither it goeth: so is every one that is born of the Spirit.*

I once had a conversation with a dear brother in the Lord, Edwin Ramirez,[107] who was nearly devoured by the woke church movement. Like me, he is Puerto Rican; but unlike me he was initially attracted to the rhetoric and focus on racial issues the woke church offered. But there was a problem. The more he got involved in the movement the more bitter he became. It got to the point where the hatred in his heart against white people—people who had never done anything wrong to him—was starting to boil over. He recalled a moment of clarity the Holy Spirit graciously gave him during the Lord's day worship service one Sunday.

> *I remember when God opened my eyes to the foolery of the woke church movement. Right around that time my wife and I had just found a church that we were just thankful that the Lord provided for us to go to. I remember singing, "Behold our God," during the worship service. And there was a point when everyone was singing to the Lord and worshipping and I kind of pulled myself back from the moment and looked around the room. I remember looking at the front and there was an older white lady singing, and I remember thinking to myself, now from a different perspective, and saying, "That's*

107 Check out Edwin's video content on YouTube: https://www.youtube.com/channel/UCS3anibvIPQc0bzc2trIEGQ

> *my sister in the Lord! That's my sister!" And I just remember weeping and thinking to myself, "Wow, God, I was so blinded that I missed the blessing of seeing, that this is my sister and I'm going to spend eternity with her and I love her."*[108]

He goes on to describe how when he was in the woke church movement he did not believe these things about white Christians. But God showed him the truth about how far he had let the root of bitterness and hatred defile his soul.

This is a great insight. It was *God* who showed him what was happening to him. It was *God* who changed his heart. God uses means, of course. God will use your arguments. God will use your efforts at bringing the scriptures in this book to bear upon the dangerous errors of the woke church. But ultimately the only person who can do the miracle of changing the hearts of those involved in the woke church is God Himself. We must pray to our King as we've never prayed before. God's will be done. He will do it.

I hope that this book has bolstered your confidence. I have had private conversations with many people who express an uneasiness with everything in the woke church. They know in their gut it is wrong; but all of their favorite authors, bloggers, and speakers seem to be going along with it. This makes many people doubt the clarity of what they thought they knew from the Bible. After all, they have seminary degrees; we do not. They are paid to teach the Bible; many of us are not. I hope this book encourages you with the fact that you are not crazy and you are not wrong. We do not

108 https://www.youtube.com/watch?v=QyD8qsbBELo

have to feel confused and dazzled by rhetoric, psychobabble, and complex nuanced arguments. The Word of God is clear.

God gave us the Bible because He wanted to be understood. The common man can understand it. You and I are fully capable of understanding the Bible and doing what it says. *We don't need permission to believe what God says.*

When an erudite, intelligent, young black woman claims to be a Christian yet stands on the stage and says, "Whiteness is wicked! It is wicked!"[109] you can simply trust the Bible that she is in sin for doing so. You simply need to follow the steps God requires of you when your brother is in sin (Matthew 18). You need not wait for your evangelical heroes to say something or do something, because chances are they agree with her and won't say anything. Even if they don't agree with her, they likely still won't say anything because the woke church has paralyzed many of our leaders in fear.

The woke church wants you to fear getting cancelled. They want you to fear being called a bigot. They want you to fear being called a racist. They want you to fear being the focus of Jemar Tisby's next horrendous blog post or editorial in the mainstream media. This fear has crippled many evangelical leaders and forced them into a position of complete submission. Do not wait for them to fight your battles for you. You will be waiting forever. The fight against the woke church will not be won with books, articles, or videos. It will be won through prayers to God and obedience to God's simple commands. Whatever everybody else decides to do, you must devote yourself to God.

---

109 https://www.youtube.com/watch?v=G7OfS_0ACWM

They will call you a bigot for refusing to accept their segregated fellowship events. Refuse anyway.

They will call you a racist for not participating with their partiality in hiring and/or scholarships and charity. Don't participate anyway.

They will call you an oppressor for not supporting their socialist welfare schemes. Don't support them anyway.

Let everybody else fear the woke church. You fear God and keep His commandments. This is the whole duty of man.

I hope you found this book helpful. God bless you!

—AD

About the Author

AD Robles is a conservative Christian living in the state of New Hampshire with his wife, three sons and ten laying hens. Using his God-given ethnicity and interest in the topic of race in the United States he has grown a popular Christian YouTube channel and podcast solely dedicated to the rise of race focused "social justice" and the "woke church." He aims to provide accessible, non-pretentious, biblical answers for people who have been made to feel as if they were deplorable for believing the Bible and loving their country.

Thank you for reading!

I would love to connect with you online.
https://gab.com/ADRobles
https://www.youtube.com/c/ADRobles
https://www.patreon.com/AD_Robles
ad@adrobles.com

Or via regular mail.
AD Robles Media
PO Box 211
Keene, NH 03431

CPSIA information can be obtained
at www.ICGtesting.com
Printed in the USA
JSHW021136231121
20691JS00002B/3